GOBLET MAKER'S WIFE

by Lonnie Pelletier

OTHER BOOKS BY LONNIE PELLETIER
Among Maya Ruins
Memory Search
Pelletier Chronicles - 500 Years
Paris Art Quest
Sea Scout Sea
Exoplanets - 101 Spacescapes
Life's Third Quarter (musical play)
My Best Screenplay (Straw Man)
Gulf Island Suite (music)
Prairie Nostalgia (music)
History Now
Robbie Phallic McKinnis (play)

Active books and paintings are shown in detail on the website:
http://LonPelletier.com

Copyright © 2018 by Lonnie P. Pelletier

All rights reserved. No part of this book may be reproduced, stored in a retrieval system, or transmitted in any form or by any means, electronic, mechanical, or recording, without the prior written permission by the author, except in the case of a reviewer who may quote passages.

    Cover design by Lonnie P. Pelletier
    Editing by Martha Todd
    Library and Archives Canada Cataloguing in Publication
    Pelletier, Lonnie, 1943 - author
    The Goblet Maker's Wife / Lonnie Paul Pelletier.
    Includes bibliographical references and index.
    ISBN 978-1928151197
    Subjects:
        1. Pelletier, Jean, 1627-1698--Historical Fiction.
        2. Pelletier, Anne, 1637-1704--Historical Fiction.
        3. Canada, France--History--1600 to 1700.

Table of Contents

	Page
Anne	9
Anne's Voyage	19
Noel - Anne's father, The Floating Home	23
William (Guillaume) - Jean's father	29
Michelle Mabille - Jean's mother	37
A Chronicle	41
Preparation For Travel	47
Voyage Initiation	51
Curt	57
The Helmsman	63
Death At Sea, But Bottom Found	67
Land	75
Battle	81
The Interview	93

The King's Girls	103
The Proposal	107
Anne's Engagement	109
Louis	121
Paul	125
Joseph	129
The Wedding	137
Marriage A La Gaumine	151
Drunken Canoeing	155
Family	159
Bliss	163
Life	167
The Dream	185
South Bank	191
Defensive Battle - Four Days	201
Next Generation	211
A Future	221
Friendship	225
Epilogue	229
Postscript	233
Appendix	242
Acknowledgments	243

It is with a great pride in family that I dedicate this book to the Pelletier and Langlois families throughout the world.

INTRODUCTION

From my early years I had the benefit of knowing about a child bride of *only twelve or so* from our family's past. This was simply a statement of fact verbally passed down over generations. As a family this was our roots, sometimes with embarrassment, but more often with pride - as we were aware that Canada had been settled by *a bunch of teenagers.*

Over the year when I had researched my novel, *Pelletier Chronicles - 500 Years,* it was obvious that both Anne and Jean were very unique individuals. It seemed necessary that I would attempt to create some substance to that history, as much of what they were confronted with, has its similarities in our modern culture.

A few of the added names and sketches of individuals other than the Pelletier and Langlois families are fictional, supplementing history as a story. The 43 reproduced subjects, sketched and painted, are all from within the seventeenth century.

The text was written in English, with an obvious understanding having to exist between the reader and the writer being necessary - as that of French being the actual idiom used by the characters.

Anne's mother, Françoise Grenier had been born about 1610 in France and the story of Anne's grandmother and her great-grandmother seemed alive. For Anne it created a relentless determination to not accept anything without questioning. She would question both church and government - later even questioning why the two were not separate.

The saga was also a lesson in both morality and an encounter with sex. In Anne's young mind the details were lost, but the overview was substantial. It was a chronical about a class system, degrading a personal worth in life and it established a necessary caution.

***

"There are cracks in the vegetable bin on the edge of the hill. There is a face peering through them. It is a woman and her eyes show her to be very frightened. It the slaughter of many people outside and she is viewing what she can of Chartres, France. It is Anne's elderly great-grandmother speaking. Dressed in rags, she is frail, but tough - tougher than the rawhide skin that seems to hang on her face."

"I know exactly how I got into this vegetable bin. Actually, I know more than just the way I crawled in. My mother told me that we always looked our worst when we were slithering into hiding, like a snake seeing something moving that could do it harm."

The younger woman is vivacious and her curves speak of her sexual charm. She is not intent on her erotic mannerisms, not consciously at least, but she is scantily dressed.

Her name is Marie. "I know that I needed to join you here, Grandma. I have breasts now. It worries me."

Anne's great-grandmother responds: "We women always had a place to hide. It was that, or being mounted by the lord of the manor."

She pauses: "Or one of his uppity ne'er-do wells. They're rough when they ride you. A good woman could always count on a slap or two on the face, whether she liked it or not - even after delivering the goods. What I hated most is when they take you in front of your family. I've always hated that. But then that is life - and in life there are those above you and well, only sometimes, there are those below you."

Marie, her granddaughter questions her: " Is it because we are women? Our men are ignored except when they're robbed?"

Anne's great-grandmother is a woman of the world, at least in her world. "It's a curse to be a bit of a beautiful woman, even a much older one like me. It's a fact of life that those above you also want to be in you. That's my experience, and that's why I hide in this bin."

Marie replied: "I was going to crawl in here with you the last time you hid. Instead I played outside. I was a little girl."

"Well my young Marie, there's a war outside but it doesn't seem to matter which side those fighting knights are on. When they see those of us lower than themselves, they take. That's why we women always had to have a place to hide."

"Grandma, is it like this for all women?"

"Maybe not everywhere. I told my grandson, that Chartres is no place for a lad like him."

She wipes off a carrot and bites into it as if contemplating a delicious morsel. "He's a good man, your brother."

She took another bite and continued: "He works hard, but he prefers to stare out at the trees and ponds. He is not a very good servant of the church, or of God or of our king. He likes to think too much. When the fighting stops, maybe I'll talk to him again."

The elderly lady looks through the wide cracks in the boards. Her eyes seen from the outside light are dimly showing her hardened character. "I'm the oldest in the family now, I have to talk to him."

Marie however, is still soft and caring as radiantly shown in her delicate tender eyes.

"The rest, well, they're all dead from work," continues the great-grandmother. "They should all leave now. I've heard that there are better places - and cleaner places - where people are not like animals."

Marie adds: "I've heard that people can grow all the food they want up in the hills."

The grandmother is being more forward: "Nobody is raped and nobody is beaten there. My family should all leave."

"I need to stay Grandmother. I have the love of my life here."

Her grandmother ignores her. "Even if our army wins this battle, we'll be okay. I guess. I'm an old lady and they won't bother me any more." She pauses: "I think they won't."

"I'll be on the outside of town with my husband someday soon." Marie pauses: "I hope."

Anne's great-grandmother explains further: "If the visiting army gets beaten back, I'll still survive. I sold most of my carrots last week and I can be eating all winter, at least this time. Anyway, no matter how it unfolds its okay. I've got vegetables to eat here. It's dark in here, but we've got vegetables. We'll just wait until we don't hear any more horses and yells."

They huddle together for a few moments, listening and not hearing anything. The great-grandmother still enjoys talking in spite of what is happening outside: "I have to stay here in Chartres. I'm too old to make a new home somewhere else."

Marie thinks that her grandmother is now rambling and changes the subject: "I guess you were born in the years of one thousand and five hundred. The priest told me that was important."

"Either way I'm just feeling old. My body gets stiff and sore when I'm scrunched up like this."

"You've lived long and well grandma."

Anne's great-grandmother replies: "I once hid away from the Lord of the Manor's son for three days. I hid on top of a haystack. He had seen me at the marketplace. My good husband could have fought him, but he would have been killed - or worse yet, we would have lost our right to toil on the land we'd been allowed on. We would have starved."

She pauses for reflection, looking out again with the eyes of fear. "All of them should just leave. I'll be talking to my grandson."

Marie is not speaking. She is looking at her hands. They are filthy with the grime of the bin and they now seem to have the look of the hands of someone her grandmother's age. Her clothes are ill fitting and obviously too tight for her age so she is constantly attempting to adjust them. She is resigned to her fate, whatever that may be.

Marie, Anne's grandmother, did marry briefly, but would share only a few weeks with her husband. He went off to war a second time and was not heard from again. The family carried on.

***

Anne's mother had related this saga often enough, it seemed like every two years. She later even vaguely remembered her great-grandmother's words. The words were always much the same, but often the meaning was more poignant, more emotional as this was not a fairy tale, nor a tale of great adventure, but it had an affect on Anne for the rest of her life.

Anne would not remember that she had been told of the three million people that had died during the French Wars of Religion. She held the belief in the chronicle in another manner. Both her grandmother and her great-grandmother were easily remembered, but she also recounted from the saga that her then younger grandmother's *love of her life* had later been slaughtered in one of the battles. It was not a general history of a nation - it was personal.

The story created the difference between naivety for a young Anne and understanding the social nuances of France. In this way she had been taught about survival. Anne was still to enjoy childhood. Her innocence was not stolen by the saga as it was simply an introduction to reality. She thought about it over the years to the extent that she needed to apply the story's shared information of those in authority not being acceptable.

* * *

Many children began training as future housewives or laborers from a relatively young age. But children were not expected to spend all day working. Her father was especially supportive of Anne's free time for *just* having fun.

Anne enjoyed *rolling the hoop*. It took place outdoors where the land was large. Anne loved it as there was plenty of room to get good and dirty. This particular game involved taking a large wooden hoop to roll. Whoever finished the fastest would win. With three sisters and six brothers she was competitive. It was also a game requiring strategy. She was best at calculating the roll of the hoop.

With only their imagination for creating games, Anne and her brothers and sisters played *leapfrog*. The girls ignored their skirts and worked at leaping over the others, but therefore it was necessary to jump higher than their brothers. Anne didn't like the game much. It was probably because her brothers would laugh at her failure. She preferred to play a game of tag.

They would go *swimming*, often in a muddy creek. They would go *fishing* after they caught their own bait. Anne's brothers prefered fishing. Due to their advantage of being more *rough and ready*, they also preferred *kIng of the castle*, and *fighting piggyback on shoulders*. Again Anne had a strategy. She coupled with one of the bigger brothers, logical as she was one of smallest - and usually was able to topple the others.

Whether they were walking or just sitting around under a tree, they enjoyed being outside. When it rained they would come inside and huddle together and play with spinning tops.

Anne's father Noel had given each of them tops, as Christmas presents. He carved them while onboard ships. Each child had a personal top and in that there was competition and fun.

When Anne was younger, they played hide and go seek. When her brothers got older and dropped out of the game, with their smaller numbers, it wasn't as much fun anymore.

Tobacco pipes were borrowed from Anne's father for blowing soap bubbles. It was great fun, but only was allowed outdoors.

They took advantage of winter and skated. Their skates were made by tying large sheep bones under their shoes to serve as runners. As usual they had no thoughts of needing skates.

In all of this Anne had a fun childhood, close family and she gained confidence. She continued in life well-rounded, wholesome and she was always proud of even her minor achievements.

Anne had blond hair, and was slight in stature; she was not to be a large woman, but had gained a resolve as she took on the adventures offered by the world around her. Her beautiful smile would be to her credit throughout her life.

ANNE'S VOYAGE

Anne left France accompanying her parents. Even at six years old, on-board the Atlantic crossing, Anne became philosophical - as she had faced the possibility of death in a very real way. She would always be able to deal with the intangible in her life, rather than day-to-day existence.

Her beliefs were consistent with her parents. She knew they were sailing in the face of God's will by venturing so far west. The crossing was against nature and it was all too likely to goad the fates into their fearsome retribution. Sea creatures were found washed up on the shore every year. Huge monstrous ocean ogres would soon be rising out of the sea and she expected it.

Onboard the intimidating vessel she was determined, as was her nature. She had bravely mounted the gangplank whispering aloud: "I can do this".

"They are beneath us somewhere", was Anne's thought as she waited for each day to end. "We only hope to be spared in having to confront them. I don't want to even see them."

She stands up with a smile and bravely states only to herself: "Yes. That's what we're doing and I will face it."

Finally in the open ocean it was not easy going. From astern, the onrushing waves with smooth faces, rear up to catch the little ship, swinging her quarters one way and then the other like a dog's wagging tail. The noise is infernal, like the roar of a landslide, as the top of a wave broke and a hundred tons of sea raced towards them, a curtain of white foam running on its face, barrelling down to then explode against the ship's deck and quarters.

The helmsman keeps the bark steady, with someone staying near him, to call the waves. The captain stands by the break to oversee the reefing. Others stand ready to tend the lines on the deck for an ongoing need to adjust the sails. The sailors move slowly and deliberately up the ratlines. About three men shuffle out along each yardarm, both port and starboard, feeling for the foot ropes as they go. They seem to be high in the clouds. Looking down, the bark is swaying sixty to seventy feet below them.

Anne fears that at any time an immense wall of water can bear down upon her family. They huddle together and hang on for their lives. Tons of freezing water often washes aboard and people are sent tumbling like matchsticks. The ship rolls until she stops falling and steadies as the keel ballast do their work. She then begins a slow heave to come upright. The masts whoosh through the air exaggerated by their angle.

Her father did not work on this ship as he often had. In the past he worked his way up within another ship's hierarchy and was known to be an expert helmsman, On this voyage he often set Anne's mind at ease with his knowledge of seamanship.

Finally walking down the gangplank, even though Anne's legs were wobbling due to her time at sea, she felt that she had survived - as she set foot on the shore of her wonderful new land. There had been no monstrous ogres, not even birds flying at them like the dragons of ancient tales. She now felt safe.

NOEL
The Home Raft

Anne's father, Noel Langlois was born on June 4, 1606 in St-Leonard-des- Parcs, Alencon, Normandie, France. He had left his home and family in 1634 in order to work on the sea. He later emigrated with them being recruited in France as a potential habitant.

Unlike other habitants, Noel volunteered his services on the ship, *the Saint Jean* at Tadoussac, Just prior to the first voyage to the New World on July 25th, he married Anne's mother Françoise Grenier.

Noel loved the sea and as a consolation he loved the great Saint Lawrence river. He sporadically returned to the sea to lead where he was best needed. He was the helmsman on two of the initial voyages bringing new settlers from France.

Noel was clearly distinguishable from other men on land by his gait. As a sailor on board a ship for extended periods, he had to learn to deal with the ship's movement as it rolled and pitched. Gaining stability by widening his stance, gave him a distinctive bow-legged appearance. Once he returned to land, he felt off-balance because the ground was no longer moving beneath his feet and he continued to sway with a swagger.

Having a problem of finances and not wishing to be enslaved to a system that he felt was usury, he combined his love of the waterways to create a farm of his own. He didn't want to be subservient to a *seigneur* (Lord of the Manor). Noel built a *floating home*.

His sense of identity did not leave him. When a helmsman, he related to his former military training. When a farmer he was able to enjoy the emotion of freedom in the new wilderness.

Being a helmsman on two ships for new immigrants, he was fully aware that most thought they were simply going to a different part of France. He knew of the ruggedness and challenges in the new land and of journeying to the other side of a vast ocean.

When Anne was born in France, her family was happy to just survive. Each day was a challenge - even for finding a meal. Coming to Canada would change that. Their local leaders had promised change and all believed that it would happen.

Noel laboured hard in the new land, initially clearing the fields for others. During this period, he built and secured a floating home with a small garden. *Secured* meant both acquired and tied up securely. The great river was not something to be taken lightly.

Living on the river also gave access to fish and meat for his wife and young family. He would daily trade his fish for the easily hunted meat of his neighbours.

When Noel had decided to move to a farm and garden that he could own, the choice seemed logical to him. The home was to be a large floating raft. As with all his neighbors, the floats of wood resembled small floating islands. They appeared to be living in town, in a natural home.

They were covered with turf and they typically had a wood hut in their centre. They wouldn't be any good out at sea as the hut could be washed away. As bateaus they seemed like a flat- bottomed type of riverboat. The concept was understandable in comparison to land farming, as the amount of acreage initially given to the habitants was minimal, not much larger than his raft.

It was a picturesque setting. Smoke was viewed, curling up from the roof of a cosy cabin, Anne and her siblings often played in front of the hut door. Their mother, Françoise would often sit and sew, while watching the waves go by when all was peaceful. Her husband could fish leisurely,

Noel Langlois guided his craft with a long pole. With this method of steerage, the entire family often pitched-in. In some cases on a river that was unpredictable, they had to.

Anne considered her new home as a floating farm yard. She observed others on land in the most positive of mind-sets. "Almost everyone on a raft has a dog or two barking." Her brothers and sisters were still left with playing spinning the tops when indoors. Fishing for her brothers became a way of life.

It was never an issue of freedom to own land. They did not contemplate the idea of land titles with clear ownership. They did not understand the concept nor was it available. Habitants were only given a *right to farm* for a minimum of a one-tenth payment of their produce.

But Noel considered the large raft to be his. He was not in any way beholden to anyone. However perceptions change and Noel had to experience life on the river before he understood the hardship created.

Two goats, four chickens, seven dogs including the pups and Noel's family - were moored on the edge of the river's bank. Summers were idyllic, at least to Noel. He had carried soil shovelled into bags and then onto his raft for the necessity of growing root vegetables. Even so, the work of toiling in a garden had the added necessity of paying attention to the great river. Especially in the three times that the raft broke away from its moorings. They then scurried about, not in panic, but with the confidence that not to far downriver they would find other moorage.

The winter brought hardship as he always feared that the ropes might let loose, catapulting them into the vicious winter's river flow. Noel had initially thought that the winter ice on the river was to be a benefit. By his calculation, it would establish a walkway from the bank to and around his raft. It didn't. He had underestimated the difference in being on the St. Lawrence river and in the less severe climate of France.

The barge consistently bobbed up and down, with a pattern surrounding it that was open water. Further the ice flows on the river were dangerous, always threatening them with collision.

* * *

They only endured one full year and it was time to move on. The barge was sold at a minimal fee, with not much to show for Noel's hard labour. Even on this small would-be-farm, labour was hard compared to the final achievement. Noel concluded that working for a seigneur might not be unbearable after all, in comparison.

Noel worked onboard a ship for another year and had been paid well for his stints as a helmsman. With money saved he bought supplies and basic agricultural tools to work on a permanent farm. He worked for a well respected seigneur, Robert Giffard and gave up on his romantic idea of living *almost as a permanent seafarer.* For the year, his family were all able to be housed by the seigneur by way of a contract.

Anne didn't remember much about the move, nor did she have a lot of memories of life on-board a raft. She only remembered it as cosy, with memories of the family being huddled in the hut, almost hugging. They often circled the wood stove for survival on this great St. Lawrence River and that meant they were physically very close. But it had also been for the reason of the eternal cold, that compelled her father to seek out the alternative.

The Langlois moved to a farm only a couple doors away from the Pelletier family. This would prove later to be significant to Anne. When Anne finally married Jean Pelletier, the boy next door, her father was known as a former helmsman and in some sense, a riverboat pilot. This reputation was a fact that he held with pride throughout his tenure as a farmer.

WILLIAM
(in French - GUILLAUME)

Sketch of William in 1653, during his time as an elected representative of Beauport, Quebec, in the Communaute des Habitants.

WIlliam's father, Jean's grandfather, Eloi was born in 1575, in France. Eloi married Francois Matte, born in the same year. Both parents, as William remembered, were not close to him in any way, typical of that century. William recounted a tale to Jean, both of family history and of attitudes; which was important to him. Family chronicles were fables to be replenished, often replacing the morality dramas and stories of the time.

***

It is a beautiful summer day on a wooded path in a forest, just outside the small town of Bresolettes, France - an area of rolling hills, treed with a dense forest and considered to be inhabited by creatures unknown.

Elio was walking cautiously while constantly looking over his shoulder for what might be on this trail, man or animal. William always added: *your grandfather, Jean*. He knew that the saga was enhanced in this way. Jean alway smiled at his father, as if to confirm the fact that it was.

One shirt was wrapped around Eloi's extra clothing, tied on a strap over his back. With a walking stick, it could be carried without impeding his pace. A wide brimmed hat, an off-white shirt, his leather hide jacket and warm wool trousers make up his wardrobe. As a robust young man he wears no sweater and his shirt was opened wide as if to demonstrate his youthful invulnerability.

He cautiously approaches a fellow traveler on the path. At a closer range he can see that he is a Monk by his garment. Elio asks: " Am I near Bresolettes? It's on a hill like that one over there, isn't it? Where everybody lives on the hill?"

The monk is curious. He has not seen a stranger for some time in these woods. "Where do you come from?"

"Chartres, where all the better homes are near the top plateau along with the church. I come from the lowest of the plateaus."

Eloi is young and naïve, giving out way too much information to a complete stranger.

The monk finally gives Eloi the answer that he has been waiting for: "Bresolettes is further on a great hill. It's a larger hill than that one."

As if to ask for it all, "Is it beside a lake?"

"It is. Why do you ask?"

Eloi continues: "I come from the water carriers, and that of the carpenters. Our bishops rule as Lords on a hill. I'm going somewhere else to learn how to live."

"Are there still Huguenot attacks in Chartres?"

"No, we won at last. But, the river overflowed and we have to rebuild the bridge on Rue de Bourg and the moat – with payment in bread, giving us nothing to trade for anything else."

"Well young man, good health and wealth in Bresolettes. I travel south."

"Good health and wealth to you. I have other plans. I will have a son there. He'll be able to read, and that son will be able to write."

* * *

The episode meant that William had passed on his own story. It was this way that history was created - and repeated. William would relate this as if it was a pledge from Jean's grandfather to the monk. It was to be a memorized chronicle for Jean and even Jean's future offspring - a pledge that the men in the family would read and write.

***

In 1619, William Pelletier had married Michelle Mabille. It is 1627, and a baby is crying - Jean. The sound comes from a small cottage. It is set on a gentle slope with a winding roadway, lightly forested on both sides. It is the Pelletier home in Bresolettes.

Jean's two older brothers are playing in the front yard area and inside a group of people are eating around a large but roughly built table. They are warmed by the massive fireplace.

Recent photo of the 1598 Pelletier Home in Bresolettes, France. Newer extensions exist on both sides.

William is entertaining his guests and making a toast with a glass of wine: "To my father Eloi - and to my sons. To my wife - and to our family's future. What we will have is better than what we had!" He waves his glass in the air in the manner of a great formal gesture.

Rural folk didn't usually toast in this manner. He had learned it from his father, as it was a learned process from a generation removed. It was learned by imitating the world of Chartres which seemed so far away. The group responds with a reply to the toast. This is an economically poor lot.

But, they are not without optimism. "To the future." Friendship has obviously replaced any feelings of inadequacy within this ragged group. Smiles are the main feature of the room.

William could hunt in the nearby forest of Perche, illegally but easily, as only a privileged few were allowed this luxury. Venison and rabbit were a treat upon occasion. This evening the gathering would enjoy venison, with poaching understandable to all.

WIlliam explained their meal further: "It is always repeated that I am a descendant of Barthelemy le Pelletier of Brittany - born in the 1300s. Barthelemy le Pelletier had been given a portion of this Perche Forest by Charles V. It was a reward for his bravery in the battle of Thouars - in 1375 yet. He was a leader and they had triumphed over the English Black Prince. I am pretending that it is in that time - that's all. I therefore hunt freely!"

William was always a verbal man and he was prone to bore his guests on many such occasions. "In 1294, another Jean Le Pelletier had been given a round stamp of 38,000 with a parcel of land. It was near Rouen, at Jumieges, near the Abbey of Junieges."

He laughed to set the pace: "In 1504, Francois Le Pelletier had taken a toll on behalf of the King of France at Loudin. We are important - we get to poach."

They all enjoy the humour as ridiculous as the logic was.

Bresolettes is surrounded by rolling hills, a beautiful area with autumn trees, winding roads and a small picturesque lake. William didn't own the house, but was able to rent the land for a long term, giving his family stability. He had then built the house.

Homes in that period normally used only sawn or squared lumber, but the Pelletier family home had solid walls made of flint- stone. Half-timbered as many homes in the area, the beams and the large fireplace hearth were the focal point.

At one end of the living area, a massive stone fireplace was built set within the entire wall. With massive rock footings being as large as the fireplace itself, this became the central focus of the entire home. The fireplace was functional allowing meals to be cooked, surrounding beds to be heated and comfort to be guaranteed.

The forest adjacent would supply all of the necessary logs for the burning fire. The fireplace is the sole source of heat during cold winter rains.

With large beams adorning the ceiling structure, a harmonious structural form of French classicism began to adorn the landscape of France. The home was on a gentle slope allowing water runoff from both rains and snow in all seasons. The pitch of the roof was ideal as the snow could not collect and seep through.

WIlliam and Michelle considered themselves happy, in this place at this time, although a source of consistent income was not readily available.

MICHELLE MABILLE PELLETIER

Michelle Mabille, Jean's mother, was the daughter of pretty Etiennette Monhe. Etiennette had died with Michelle's birth. Michelle had been baptized at Saint-Aubin church in Tourouvre, arrondissement of Mortagne, France, on May 20, 1592. With her father William and grandfather Jehan, Mabille lived in the parish of the Poterie only a few kilometres to the east. Their occupation described their poverty.

Her grandfather only had one means of gathering money. He would search in the streets for coal that had been spilled or dropped. Sweeping it up with his only tool, a shovel, he then enthusiastically hoarded it to sell to various tenants and homeowners. This provided very little in substance for enjoyable life.

But in her youth, Michelle refused to become downtrodden, believing that her future would turn out better. It was an irony that Michelle would later marry a merchant of charcoal.

On February 12, 1619, Michelle Mabille married William Pelletier at the church of Saint-Aubin in Tourouvre, only seven kilometres east of Bresolettes. WIth a pursuit of better opportunity in selling charcoal, made and taken from the hills and sold to the town-folk of Tourouvre, they logically moved away from their picturesque Bresolettes home.

William and Michelle found their new home near Tourouvre, to be named *La Gazerie*, an appealing name. William bought it outright and acquired a title. The name implied a home of substance, an estate. In actual fact the house wasn't near to being an estate. It was a warm and dry shack with warmth being a positive fact.

Their wedding was a simple celebration. Food and drink was the main theme for these families. They did not eat well, but whatever they had they shared. Potatoes grew well in the area. Wine could be made. They enjoyed a wine of dandelions, root vegetables and anything that might ferment.

Michelle was a strong-willed woman, at least she dominated over William. He did become his own person after the birth of his three sons, but needless to say, being older she held the upper hand. William was born in 1598, making him five years younger. In rural France, it was not unusual for couples to have a large age difference. Even so, it was nice to think about love at weddings.

In moving to Tourouvre in 1630, William began working at the trade of charcoal merchant. He had a partner in the venture. Like many partnerships it was not equal and they parted ways.

From his one-time partner, Jehan Maunoury, he acquired one hundred and six cords of wood to make charcoal for Mace Guyot and Antoine Pichon. Guillaume and Jehan delivered one hundred and seventy-five pipes of charcoal and four pistoles d'or. As payment, they had the right to cut six more cords of wood for their ongoing business. As WIlliam's business was a registered fact in writing, he was showing to all that he did read and write within the family promise. A paper trail in rural France was uncommon.

Michelle contemplated that for most of William's work, he was paid by barter. This was not lucrative in any way. She was always looking for other possibilities.

Tourouvre's class structure could be generalized into three sections. The upper class or nobility consisted of appointed officials, royal administrators, wealthy landowners, upper clergy members, and army officials. They were followed by the bourgeoisie: the merchants, traders, shopkeepers and tradespeople. The farmers and fishermen made up the lowest social strata.

Michelle took great pride in knowing that her husband was a merchant, *almost a bourgeoisie* - all with a pride in his literacy. If anything described Michelle it was the fact that she understood well the idea of conserving cloth. She had grown up in abysmal poverty but looked forward positively to a new life in distances afar.

At the time of the decision to move to New France, she was in complete control of being dependent on the clothing that they would take with them. It could not be replaced in her future new home, only resewn. On her journey she planned to carry a pack-sac, made of cloth, stuffed tightly with as many rags and clothing as she could find.

William and his wife sold a part of their land to Robert Loyseau and leased their property for five years to Jean Rousseau, their brother-in-law. The rent was fifteen livres. In addition, they made Rousseau their agent so they could leave the area on their escapade to a new and very unknown part of France. It never occurred to them that they were going to a different country.

Michelle could not read or write. She practiced until she could sign her name. It was as a matter of pride within her literate family. As a woman, she was comfortable with her husband making any decisions that involved the use of written words.

Often *Readers* would tour the small towns of this part of France, much like the minstrels of song. They offered their stories for listening, along with their books for sale. Michelle and William could enjoy hearing the stories, even without making any purchases of the very expensive books. It was a given that in their future, Michelle's maturity and her willingness for hard labour was more important than being able to read.

A CHRONICLE

In his first young years after their move to Tourouvre, Jean had been given his own chronicle of morality by his father. It was in this manner that a history of family seemed to be repeated. Jean knew that he would also relish in retelling the story to his sons.

***

"It is a cloudy morning, cold and the miserable winter had set aside the feeling that spring was possible in the dark air. A lone horseman is riding between Bresolettes and Tourouvre. The pathway, once used mostly by foot traffic, is now being used by mule and cart. The imagined scene seems familiar as it was parkland and rolling hills.

The year is 1640. The voice of William rings out in this French countryside. He was thrown by his horse and is lying next to a slough, swearing. His horse has done that which it has been trained to do. It stops dead in its tracks as soon as its rider has dismounted – no matter what the circumstance. When the neck reins drop, the beast takes the action as a signal to come to an instant stop and remain stationary. This is not a noble mount. It is the opposite of a glorious stallion, but it is transportation and it is a trained family pet.

An approaching monk from the Trappist monastery at the neighbouring village of Soligny is walking in the opposite direction and he stops to help him up.

"Are you okay?" The monk looks at his left hand.

Even though William had been thrown off his horse, he maintains something tightly in his fist. "What is it you're harbouring there?"

William looks down at his map and gives a reply that seems close enough to an answer. "Good, the map is still readable. My dumb father-in-law will be able to see his daughter's destination on a map. He couldn't understand how she was trying to travel so far, or even where it all might be."

"A map? What kind of map? That's very unusual. Why are you travelling?".

"It's a chart of the New World." William answers rather proudly.

The monk understands the issue of the chart, but does not understand the concept of a new community elsewhere. "Do you need it?"

William ignores him, "Dam. My father Eloi learned to read and write. Why can't my father-in-law understand our simple contracts? They're an obligation to travel and work here. See, it's on the map."

William points to the map with his other free hand. The monk knows that as clergy he was supposed to be seen as wise.

"Father-in-laws are meant to be our Lord's by virtue."

William somehow feels that he should explain: "It's for my beautiful Michelle - her father demands to see a map before he blesses our excursion into an unknown world."

The monk laughs. He now understood the situation. "Of course, life isn't meant to be easy!"

Recent photo of the original Bresolettes Church

William takes the opportunity to talk. He needs to voice his frustrations. "In Bresolettes, to enter our church, you cross through the cemetery. But me, I need a future."

William explains further, "My present life is focused entirely on a story of death and life everlasting. But I want a future, not just a past."

The monk is a philosopher. He attempts to look wise and looks off into the horizon. He then says: "Over and over again the peasants here have seen their fields and homes laid to waste by the laid-off soldiers returning from war. These guys live off the countryside, wandering about plundering at will. They make the Lords add even more taxes for our protection from them."

He sighs in an animated manner: "This is during when the Lords only sometimes feed them. When they don't, we all end up feeding them from our produce."

He pauses and turns to William: "You know, we had civil war for almost forty years, when I was born."

William shakes his head to the negative: "That's why I'm leaving. I'm a member of a merchant's guild in town, but there's still the new bourgeoise - a lazy and elite middle class forming right before our eyes. They control. I'll go and serve my king and country afar."

He pauses and looks at his hands. "Anyway, I'm not hurt."

The monk seems to show an effeminate side in his manner. It was possibly apparent as to the reason as he asked his next question: "You're married then?"

William ignored any indications of the reason for the monk's tolerance: "I left Bresolettes to marry Michelle at the St.-Aubin Church at Tourouvre. She was born in 1592 - that's almost six years older than me."

They both smile, enjoying the candid communication.

William continues: "We met as we were celebrating the feast of John the Baptist. We were running through the fields on the hills near here, with flaming torches and we were rolling burning wheels. It was a wonderful festivity. I remember that we both enjoyed it - and that's when we first met."

The monk nods: "You sound like you have your mate."

"She isn't even afraid of the wild animals from the dark forests that we know are prowling at night. You know, we don't even know them all, or what they're called. There are a few monsters out there! She's a good one to embark on any journey with."

The monk was saying good-by: "Well God be with you and your kin!"

William is excited about his major trip. He had journeyed no more that ten kilometres away from his home in his entire life. He wants to tell this monk more: "Over eighty families are intent on going! There's war everywhere else so we'll be okay. If nothing else it will be peaceful!"

The monk smiles very knowingly with his hands hidden and arms crossed within his loosely hanging sleeves.

"We've had two young children die on us. Jean's left to us though. He'll be okay and he's a strong lad."

The monk is interested and did not comment on the tragedy: "I've heard of the new world!"

"You know there are only sixty European people in all of New France! They need us over there!"

William gets on his horse. He turns and waves goodbye and rides away, speeding up quickly into a cantor.

* * *

One of three sons, Jean had been baptised where his parents were married in the church of Saint-Aubin in Tourouvre, France.

His two brothers Claude and Guillaume were baptized there in February, 1622.

PREPARATION FOR TRAVEL

17th century French museum piece - photo by Lonnie Pelletier

The year is 1640 and William stands beside the family cart. Jean had enjoyed a childhood at a time when the early death of two brothers was normal.

Jean, now thirteen, often questioned his father about the trip as he couldn't get enough details. The problem was that there was little information to be had. WIlliam knew that his family was about to travel into the unknown.

William turns to his cart and hits it on the side. "With this we don't walk. It's not so bad being a coal merchant when you own a mule and cart. It'll only take us eight days to the port of La Rochelle. We sail to new France from there."

Jean is calculating. "If we can sell it there before we sail."

"It has a five-foot box, with sides that extend to five feet high. Look at its fourteen spoke hardwood wheels. We have something great to sell! We'll have money when we arrive at our destination!"

Jean laughed. He had never seen his father as excited: "You sound like a would-be charlatan, Dad."

William ignores the remark. He has always served the community with hard labour. He is simply enjoying the life changing event.

"I'll easily trade the mule, the cart and even some coal thrown into the cart for good luck - in exchange for light tools and warmer clothing. That's after we arrive at the port. We'll be ready!"

Jean says: "We'll be needing faith in the Lords that control us from Paris for this adventure. Those above us must not fail."

William is positive: "I have always trusted those in charge of our destinies. They are all good men, I'm sure."

"I have much to learn - have no answers," Jean pondered.

"You'll be learning about the smoking of fish, son. They've already learned it and more, from the local Mi'kmaq Indians. That's what the recruiters, the Juchereau brothers told us. What's more, my brother Antoine has said that he's coming too."

Jean is sceptical as typical thirteen-year old would be: "So we at least eat."

William speaks with excitement. The reports that he had now received may have been only rumours, but they were all very positive. "And we'll also have garden! We'll leave as soon as your mother's parents get well."

Jean is still attempting to gather details: "How exactly will we earn a living there?"

"We'll work for a good seigneur, and I know of him. Some apparently aren't so good, but he has a good reputation. He's Robert Gillard and he owns the grant near Quebec City, a part of France."

"Well, so who pays for it? The journey, I mean."

"Since our last meeting with the recruiter, I've learned who, and I can tell you. It's Cardinal Richelieu in Paris. He came up with the idea of the *Company of the One Hundred Associates*. They invest as a group and we do the work. But let me tell you my son - we also receive a home, food and good clothing! Life on a seigneury is better than here. We can become a habitant with certain rights by simply relocating and working hard!"

"And I can finally serve King and God. Whatever happens will happen!" Jean makes the statement, knowing it is really a question.

William experienced financial hardship in Tourouvre, but it was not due to bad management. He sold his charcoal easily. The problem was that he was often obliged to sell with promissory notes.

He now sold his right to his home by way of a promissory note through a trusted friend, Jean Rousseau, as the acting agent, The leftover money could later be used by William, towards an actual purchase of another right to farm. But William was aware that he might never receive the money. He felt he had nothing to lose and everything to gain by sailing over the vast ocean and taking a chance.

On March 8, 1641, after waiting for the deaths of both Michelle Mabille's father William and of William's father Eloi, the family left Tourouvre for the journey to New France. The intention was to leave in 1640 catching the first ship crossing, but they had waited for the second ship, with an expectancy of death. Being with their fathers in their last days was more important to them. Jean was now fourteen years old.

VOYAGE INITIATION

1641 Sailing - by the Pelletier family
Acrylic on canvas board by Lonnie Pelletier

On May 7th, 1641, the 120-ton ship, Rene des Sables, prepared to leave LaRochelle to make haste for the destination of Quebec. The scene at the port of La Rochelle is hurried. It is with a pace never before seen by the Pelletier family. To them La Rochelle was a large city, one they found foreign in every way.

They had bartered their belongings as William had promised, but not for the amounts he had hoped for. But having bartered well enough, the family, which included Jean's Uncle Antoine, now would carry baskets, small utensils, clip-on ice skates and a few coats.

The Pelletier family were not yet in view of the dock due to buildings surrounding them, higher than they have ever seen before, some three floors high. When clear of the buildings, they turn the corner of a narrow street, as they make their way down to the dock. All four see the ship for the first time with outright astonishment.

To them, it is a ship from other worlds. Approaching it cautiously they look up at its six-story high sails. Upon nearing the gangplank to the awaiting ship, they are entering a very strange world.

William tries to sound in control. This is surprising beyond belief for a man from a rural French hillside community and he is stammering: "It's one of the frigates of the harbour. I've been told that for over one hundred years…" He is then interrupted.

Curt, a small but muscular sailor, approaches the group from the side. He startles them, both by appearing suddenly, but also by speaking in the language of the sea: "I'll let ye know your directions, me mates! Follow me! They calls me Curt!"

He had shouted as if they had approached him from a country that did not share his language. He knew that they would not understand his unique dialect.

They follow him up the gangplank onto the ship.

Curt is taking control of the situation and he continues, not even waiting for a response: "Me captain tol' me to help ye. Here's how it goes: *Aft* means towards the stern or rear - right? *Forward* means towards the bow or front of the vessel."

He again laughs in his likeable manner. "*Aloft* refers to anyplace in the masts, yards or rigging. *Astern* is behind to stern - right? *Athwartships* is across the boat. *Below* refers to anyplace under the main deck - right? Ye got that?"

Curt bellows with laughter, as in these moments he is in his glory - he has a chance to show off his knowledge. It is ordinarily a trade ship, with cargoes of fish and he rarely speaks with strangers.

Michèle observes that the deck is slippery and soiled with gobs of tobacco juice spit. She tries not to make a face.

Deckhands are now busying themselves hoisting bags aboard, reefing lines through blocks, tarring the shrouds and reaming up deadeyes.

She shrugs assuming all of this is logical and has decided not to speculate on details. She is sure that bravery would be her duty and if not they wouldn't even get off land. A transition was necessary. Michèle feels a chill of anxiety as she walks across the deck of the rocking boat. She is uneasy and they haven't even left the dock. To her the men smell unlike a farmer after a day's hard labour, but more like salted pork that is long past its usefulness. *It is certain that below deck was not going to be any better.*

Curt carries on as their tour guide: "*Poop* is a small raised deck near the stern. *Port Quarter* is on the left, facing forward. *Quarter* is the side of the vessel from midships extending to stern. *Starboard Quarter* is on the right, facing forward."

Laughing again he motions them to go straight down to their cabin. "Just go down over there with your stuff. Ye can then stand back up here to watch the land sink away after." He understood how dark it was below the deck.

Curt points to the opposite side of the ship. "Ye'll be standin' over there when ye come back up - out of our way."

Curt continues laughing. He is a likeable fellow by all accounts.

Anthony looks at William and they give a shrug and a laugh in agreement. A need for a sense of humour is obvious.

As they continue to the hatchway Curt says: "You might be spending most of your time below decks during sail."

Jean asserts himself: "I was wanting to volunteer services on deck."

Curt replies: "We'll see. You'll see if you want to later."

Having walked over to the railing, Michèle gazed out to sea. "It looks deep – very deep." She is thinking of the rolling hills and forests that they had left and how welcome they would be if she could walk through them again.

Jean joins her and voices one of his concerns: "It's the creatures under it that stir the imagination. They must be even wilder than anything found in our dense forests."

Michèle says: "I'm told that we are to ignore them and they'll ignore us. We are also to pray for our passage around them. I've heard that repeatedly."

William had walked a few feet from their side, observing everything he could not control. He joins them and makes his suggestion. He has always been a firm father and logical husband. "Let's find our bedding quarters. We have a passenger number - it shows which bunk to sleep in."

CURT

Many of the sailors were not keen on washing, and a deodorant could be made from barks and wood. An advice book of 1547 suggested that after getting out of bed and stretching, you coughed, spat, and defecated.

"Then you put your breeches on, comb your head and wash your hands, wrists, face, eyes and teeth with cold water. A really fastidious person might clean their teeth with burned rosemary wood, to *make the teeth white and drive out the worms in them*, which as everyone knows causes holes and toothache."

Curt had not read the book.

Jean soon discovered that Curt was available for questions and he took advantage of it. Jean presumes that this would be his only time onboard anything like this. Curt consistently waved his arms and pointed in many directions as he spoke to Jean, even as they usually sat on one of the cargo boxes on deck.

"She's called a Caravel. She's a cargo vessel displacing about two hundred tons. She's rigged with three masts and a bowsprit, lateen sails with frequently used square sails on the fore masts - along with a spritsail. She's gaff rigged with a four-sided mainsail. A halyard hoisted controls each sail. She's rigged with up to three masts - with a mizzen-mast stepped on the transom with the mizzen sheeted to a boomkin. She's also rigged with lateen sails, so we can sail close to the wind."

Jean is the kind of young person that enjoyed any communication from his questions. He had discovered that adults easily relate to youth, if the young show a need for their knowledge or wisdom. "It's my future, you know – with the strangeness of things to come. We were going to sail last year on the 1640 sailing - but we waited for relatives to die or something like that."

Jean wanted to ask about the strange words that Curt was using. Instead he thought of his family that had died in the last few years. Jean then looked around at the hustling men.

"They're all busy. How many are there?

Curt answered: "It takes fewer than twenty seamen aboard."

"Who's the youngest?"
"It's our eleven-year old sea-boy and the oldest is the sixty-year old boson cook. How old are you my boy?"

"Fourteen. My father is forty-three and my mother is forty-eight. My uncle Antoine is the youngest in my father's family."

Their conversation was interrupted by the captain's shouts. He gave orders to the sailing master, from the top deck - loud and clear: "Hail sheets and get the barque moving!"

Almost immediately sea chanteys are heard from forward as the jacktars went about their practiced duties, shaking out topsails and courses and hoisting a pair of jib sails. As they pulled out into open water, the towline fell off from the wharf and the sails came home, filling up with the magical wind.

The captain is formally dressed, in a brocade long-coat, silken hose and buckled shoes, as is his first mate. The first mate wears the same costume as his master except for its colour and ornamentation, which was one scale lower. They are bareheaded with hair tied in a pigtail with a miniature bow. Later the captain would often wear a traditional wig.

The captain shouted to the sailing master: "Snug her down good and tight with hatches battened and all loose gear stowed in good and proper order. Careful as she goes men."

The initial few days of the voyage go by without event. For the rural folk aboard it can be said that all was unusual, however these days were smooth sailing.

Within two days, Jean begins to write in a dairy as he doesn't want to forget the unique words that everyone seems to be using. He develops a habit of sitting on the deck with his back against the railing, where it is easy enough to find a spot where he can sit out of harm's way. The men seem to only work higher above the deck, as they focus on the set of the sails and all that it involved. Jean is proud of his new vocabulary of the sea and the diary was very forgiving if he gets it wrong.

"We most often plough through the sea, in ever changing fashion under topsails and two jib sails. Ever so often she lifts her stern to a long ocean swell running under the keel, barrelling up at a tremendous speed such that the bark was yawing about like when my father broke a wheeled cart. Overhead, the topmast groans at the trestle trees, where they're joined to the lower masts."

Jean is honest in his writing: "This adds to my own nagging worry about gear failure, with the sails tumbling down. A bight of loosened canvas, caught by a gust, can render a man insensible or knock him clean off the yardarm."

He had added: "It was often as if the bark has been picked up by a giant's hand, to be played with like a toy. At other times swells would be heaping up to the height of a house then lifting us high as a swell roared under her stern, she would smash against the rudder blade as the helmsman struggled against the wheel's kick."

Jean continues, putting his sentence in capital letters: "WE WOULD THEN SCRAMBLE DOWN THE COMPANIONWAY TO COMPLETE DARKNESS BELOW DECK."

He attempts to relate all of his emotions about sailing to an unknown reader ashore: "Often the outcome is tattered sails streaming in the wind. Lines and reefing pennants thrashed and snaked wildly, smashing blocks and clattering against the masts. Broken yards hang askew and upper ratlines droop slack and lifeless. Shrouds are frayed to threads with much of the rigging gone. Work is then simply scheduled to refurbish all that is broken. Land has to be reached in some manner."

Curt approaches Jean while he is writing, as usual in a friendly manner: "How're ye doin' Mate?"

"Okay." Jean pauses for a moment to think about what he really wants to ask: "What's between us and where we're going? Anything?"

Curt says: "Ahead and to the north lays a vast shore marked on sea-charts only as *Terra Incognita*. There's vast lands of either islands or continents and no one is certain."

He pauses, then explains further: "Dead reckoning can be in error by many leagues. We'll be forced to sight landmarks near arrival."

Jean replied: "I saw a chart of the new lands of France."

Curt is being honest: "That's just a sketch son."

Jean voices another concern: "Have we got food?"

"We might have rotten food soon. After the first few days we depend on the rancid food in the barrels lashed outside of the galley. It'll usually be dried eels, salted fish and some beef. But this sailing we've got some fruits and spices for later."

"So we're in good shape for this trip?"

Curt knew there was one thing that he hadn't made clear. "When the weather gets rougher again, the port lids will be closed. Your tiny cabin'll be a bit dark or cold. For your safety, we might have to lock you in for a bit. You'll be okay."

The North Atlantic wind increased: The masts arch across the sky as the sailor's hands claw at the heavy wet canvas with freezing fingers struggling to tie off the reefing pennants, while the wind whips at the lines. Once they tame the foresail with a reef, halving the spread of canvas, the ship rides easier. They can descend from the foremast to struggle along the heaving deck to mount the mainmast and continue reefing there in what seems to be an unending battle between men and the wet cold elements.

Jean thought of the little light that they would have down below decks, but more importantly he was aware of the lack of air circulation. The dead air accumulated a stench that he had never experienced before.

THE HELMSMAN

Days go by slowly, and each is greeted with enthusiasm by everyone on board. It was as if each sunrise or sunset marks the land being just that much nearer. Each day is also a mark of a twenty-four hour period that won't have to be repeated.

Jean visits the crew as often as he can, however, he soon finds out that with the exception of Curt and the helmsman that no one wants their work interrupted. It never occurred to him that the sailors simply considered him to be a *wimp from the hard* (land). He especially enjoys talking to them both.

Perhaps due to the helmsman having kin ashore in Jean's age group, or perhaps just due to the vast age separation, the helmsman is always willing to speak with him. Jean doesn't know which reason existed in the helmsman's mind, but he concludes that it doesn't matter.

Jean uses the opportunities to his benefit. "Mr. Langlois - hi. May I speak with you again? I sure learned a lot last time."

The helmsman smiles with a firm facial expression of concentration and nods his head to the affirmative.

The helmsman keeps the bark steady at the wheel, with someone staying to call the waves. Jean had made his study of seamanship count and when in lighter seas he was allowed to assist. He would stand proudly to the port side and give the necessary extra readings of the waves to the helmsman at the wheel.

Mr. Langlois had given Jean an ultimate compliment: "You are calling the waves with the best of them."

Jean smiles and continued to take advantage of this opportunity at sea: "Many of the colonists are sick and weak. The common wants of nature isn't possible to them any longer."

The helmsman shrugs. "We just surge forward. That's what we do."

Jean says: "There's a great stench below. But I finally got it right. When I go to the weather railing, I'm reminded to protest to the lee side - never to windward. So far I've not barfed down below."

The helmsman laughs and says: "Like a cathedral gargoyle you can open your mouth wide like a yawn -- and release the putrid stream of juices and pottages from the bottom of your stomachs – but only if you make it up to the outer deck. Then you feel a lot better. It's the obvious cure."

Jean goes on: "The between-deck areas are like a dungeon when the hatchways are locked. When the hatchways are finally opened, steam rises and the stench is like from a pigpen. The air becomes so foul that my friends are often driven to the upper deck, in spite of risking the rush of water across our ship's deck."

The helmsman is calm in his manner and easy to like in spite of his concentration to follow his captain's orders. "I know - the few beds are also in a dreadful state. The straw, once wet with seawater, soon rots. Did you know the boy that just died?"

"Yes Sir. He was sort of a neighbour."

The helmsman explains: "We'll be giving him a proper conveyance to the railings. We have him sewed up in canvas. Go along then. They'll do the funeral service. The winds and the waves are calm enough."

The Captain then shouted orders to his men: "Set the foresail as being of a *broach to*. It is an offering to God."

Everyone onboard stands in a double row on the deck, each holding a burning candle. The body wrapped in canvas, is carried along the line of individuals, accompanied by the priest as he chants. Each person touches it as a parting gesture.

The priest reads the service in Latin while often discreetly balancing himself as he stands to the side and holds on to the rail. The deceased is then slid down the plank that had been laid across the ship's railing.

Jean watches this final act as the body falls into the sea. He can't help but think of how the splash seemed insignificant in the ocean's vastness. He gives an explanation that is half prayer, half statement: "God".

Curt sidles up to Jean and speaks quietly: "The bodies are always buried from the starboard side. They slip into a bottomless sea. It's better than a land burial, it's forever bottomless here."

Jean looks out at the ocean expressionless: "The body could have been mine."

Not coincidental within the settlement of a small population - the helmsman was to become Jean's father-in- law.

DEATH BUT BOTTOM FOUND

"Storm At Sea", from a sketch by Ebenezer Wake Cook

The next day is rough seas with heavy rain. Another burial is needed. The deaths are starting to mount up now and both sickness and dying are becoming a way of life. Both wind and rain are slapping against their faces as the group congregates on deck.

The helmsman shouts out an explanation to Jean: "It is accepted that some of the semblance of a ceremony can be set aside. Extra canvas can't be spared and rough waters disallow the norm."

Jean moves to stand beside his mother. He leans closer to her and speaks with authority to her on the matters that he now has learned: "I'm glad we haven't set the foresail as being of a possible broach-to. That would be a normal gesture, but the wind's from the side. In high winds a broach-to set of the sail is dangerous." Curt and the helmsman have taught him well.

Her reply is simple: "I'm sick."

Jean holds her hand as a young man would, well past his actual fourteen years.

All the members observing the funeral ceremony are hanging on to railings or anything that is secured. Water is washing over the deck soaking their feet - as each individual attempts to show a brave face.

* * *

A lookout has been scheduled in spells, and the sailors swap their time throughout the day in order to keep alert. As they close in on the new continent, they are also to look for chunks of blue-grey ice. Some of the pieces are the size of a small boat and are broken half-melted floes or pieces knocked off from larger icebergs.

Smaller ones battering the forepart of the hull produce a constant and unwelcome drum sound, destroying any possibility of a full night's sleep. In the New World and around the Gulf of St. Lawrence, the sea-ice cracks in April and loosens in May. It floats free in June; thus the timing of the voyage had been critical.

As they approach the coast, fog is to be expected. Heavy mists roll down to envelop them in a clammy soup, obscuring the sun, the sky and even the sea so very near to them. Each day it is hoped that the fogbanks would lift by noon. When they didn't it seems like a consolation that heavy winds are not the order of the day.

The settlers are willing to take whatever weather they are given. Heavy winds often mean that they made better time, but the sea would then swell to wash onto the deck and create their hell. They often discussed the pros and cons of high seas versus an ocean like glass. However, they accepted that they had no control.

* * *

Jean's diary has become important to him now as he did not want to forget this journey. He sits in his spot on the deck and continues to write: "When having to go aloft, the men had developed a system as they lost sight of each other halfway up the ratlines. They worked together by using their shouts and chanteys. When they sing, it is like eerie sounds descending from the clouds above"

As Jean begins to go below decks to stow his diary, he hears a shout. Perched high at the main-topsail, a seaman cups his hands to yell out. He points to the horizon: "Land there!"

A second seaman quickly goes to the port side with a long line dragging in the sea. He shouts: "No bottom found." He pauses between shouts for a minute or more, then shouts again: "No bottom found." It is repetitious: "No bottom found."

Everyone has gathered on deck with an expectation of something that they really don't understand.

Finally the call: "Bottom found, eighty fathom, small shingle and slate stones."

A cheer goes up that blends into the waves and the wind in a majestic manner.

Two days later, having followed the sight of shore, they sail into a large river mouth. Indians with canoes come alongside with their daily catch, both smoked and fresh, which they offer to exchange for biscuits and pork by way of their shouting in their unknown language.

Curt has now sidled up to Jean. He is often a friend by his side.

Jean, turns to him: "How did they catch them?"

Curt explains: "The fish were caught in wicker baskets shaped upon stakes stuck into the sand within the tidemark."

"Here? In the great St. Lawrence River?"

Curt says: "Everything comes from this river. We travel on it, we eat from it - and we often fear it."

"We fear it? We're most happy to finally see it."

Curt laughs: "We're seeing it before winter freeze-up. It can be a sight that's not so welcome."

Jean, as always has another question: "So how do they catch fish in a basket?"

"The baskets have two entrances, one pointing up the river, the other pointing down. These have no doors but have sharp pointed wands to prevent the fish from exiting as they head into the basket."

"I'll try that someday soon."

Curt smiles and says: "I know you will. It's the Indians that will teach you to how to survive. They'll teach all of us how to survive."

As the small ship journeyed up the St. Lawrence River, Jean and his father and mother stand together by the railings edge. They are in awe at their first close look at the new land.

Upon sighting the wharf, their ship is joined by two launches taking their towlines out bow and stern to keep their craft on station. Their boat is able to drop their jib sail and let the staysail sheet go free as they move alongside the wharf with precision. This requires much coordinated skill. The crew get it right the first time, not having to make a second or third pass by the dock. With master mariners such as these, it seems easy.

Having been secured to the wharf with ropes tied down, the seamen settle the bark. They busy themselves with folding the sails, boxing the yards, and coiling-down the lines. The chaos and activity is both loud and hurried. Everyone seems aware that concentration is now on a change in activity, other than being under the control of the sheets of kite in the wind. The change in focus is very welcome to the Pelletier family and their neighbours - it is land based.

After what seems to be a very long wait, the four members of the Pelletier family, William, Michèle, Jean and Antoine, begin to walk down the gangplank. They walk as if they are uncertain that the boards might collapse. But the real reason is that the next steps of their life would be onto a very new home. In that there is much uncertainty.

Michèle cupped her hands to her cheeks. She yelled out: "My god we are actually here!"

WIlliam was smiling and much more deliberate: "We were meant to be here - and here we are."

Michèle continues. She is bubbling with excitement and relief: "We've sailed forever. Do we really know where we are? Is it a good place?"

"Look at it all. All was brown where we departed. Here everything is green. It has to be a good place." Guillaume is laughing with every breath.

Jean speaks to his father with a wide grin: "You said to trust those who control us. It is to be good."

Jean turns to Curt who is standing to the side at the top of the gangplank, waiting to say goodbye: "I'll not forget my lessons at sea, Curt."

Curt smiles and replies: "I'll try to remember that I've been on salt provisions this time. I always drink too much fresh water - all at once, in the first hours on shore."

Jean is still asking questions: "Always? Why is that so bad?"

Curt is happy as usual to explain: "I then get six weeks of dysentery until I return to the sea. So far, I've never gotten to know the exotic shores onto which I've traveled."

Jean shows he understands: "So you've seen many a bottom of a bucket - on many a port; but you've not seen the ports?"

Curt laughs: "That's it my friend. Just the bottom of those buckets."

Jean returns to the top of the gangplank and Jean and Curt shake hands. Jean looks back and waves in parting as the three of the Pelletier family place their feet on land for the first time in three months.

As always, the fourth more silent member, Antoine, is happy to trail behind.

LAND

They stop on the dock and buy bread from a vendor. It's fresh and due to this drastic change of diet, it tastes as rich as any cake. Conversation is lively as they check in with the local administrators that have been patiently waiting for them.

As they began to walk on the dock area, William yells back to Antoine: "I'm told we're now two hundred and forty Europeans in New France!"

Antoine asserted: "The guy back there said that even after one year of clearing the land, many tree stumps still remain."

Another administrator approached them. Within the chaos of this landing, of what seemed like everyone scrambling to set foot on shore at once, he had more positive news. He had heard Antoine's statement of wanting to labour and wanted to add to his idea of new fortunes: "The total produce was eight barrels of wheat, two barrels of peas and three barrels of corn. It's plentiful by all of our standards."

Jean is now excited with having devised a new plan as he looks around the dock. They are on the river, but the hills of large green trees dominate. "So now we can work for the company. We can work in wood. You know - this really is the place for it."

***

On October 5, 1642, William had sent a letter from New France, back to his agent Jean Rousseau. A second friend and former neighbour volunteered his service for its complicated and lengthy delivery. Upon returning to Tourouvre, France, his friend Mathurin Gagnon was successful.

William and Michèle were overjoyed when they finally heard of the almost impossible delivery. Mail such as this was not always received by the intended recipient. If it was delivered it was usually to the wrong person. The focus of the letter shown in its body was stated as: "In order to resolve family and business matters and division of the Pelletier property..."

After the division of the property with Jean Rousseau as the acting agent, forty-five livres was paid to Francois Choiseau on behalf of William. This was for both a past debt and a token for the past service that was covered in this letter. It was a written venture flaunting the availability of an actual paper trail and more importantly the leftover money could be used by William, towards an actual purchase of the right to farm in two years.

The money from France was put towards a purchase of the *right to farm*. They had secured their two potential farm plots and were visiting the site. Standing within earshot of the roar of Montmorency Falls added to that powerful moment of walking on their land for the first time. Their applications for land, along with their negotiations, produced positive results.

Standing in his own field for the first time, William with a wide smile declared: "In less than our three-year contract - we've become habitants. Our initial contract of promise for only hard labour is now set aside." He is referring to himself and Antoine, but he likes to not exclude Jean, now fully grown at seventeen.

Jean asks: "What does that really mean? What's in it for my life here?"

Antoine, Jean's very close uncle, is firm and serious in his belief: "We're no longer just immigrants or *colons* and we can work on our own dwellings now. To be a habitant means to be a free farmer - means we have secure roots."

William holds up one of their documents and reads: "Giving the rights to William Pelletier from - the formal owner, Martin Grouvel in the Seigneury of Beauport..."

He pauses and smiles at Jean, then continues: "This establishes a six-acre frontage, between the St. Lawrence River and the Montmorency River."

Antoine says: "That puts the Antoine Pelletier farm to the west of Montmorency Falls." He pauses, turns and looks behind him. "And that's where I intend to stay."

Jean says: "You know, it's a lot more than we had in the old country back there. This is our new stand. I'll take up some land as soon as I have a family of my own."

Michèle has been back at the wagon and their oxen. She approaches them with a basket of food. She is also all smiles: "You new habitants need food just the same."

With his rejuvenated enthusiasm, Jean wants to provide the explanation: "It's the right to use, just for us Mom. This is our place in this world."

Michèle says: "When we sailed over, I wondered if this existed. Now all of our work and that trip of pure hell seems to give us something very real."

Jean turns to his father: "What more do we pay?"

William replies: "Seigneurial dues once per year - on the day of the *Planting of the Maypole*. It's a festivity. We show loyalty and honour to the seigneur then, but it's not like the peasantry or paysans in France. We'll gather at his manor house. We may even soon have committees with elected local representatives."

Jean asks: "But do we know how much we pay?"

Antoine interjects: "It's reasonable, the payment is a few bushels of wheat per year. And we grind our flour at his mill for very little added cost."

WIlliam continues: "The seigneur will let us use his rights of hunting, fishing and water. If we ever sell our right to farm, only one-twelfth of the land value as tax will be due to him."

Jean is delighted: "We're obviously here to stay."

Antoine turns to address Jean, fatherly at most times: "As the only surviving son, you are an adult with the handicap of great expectations." They both laugh.

They prepare and enjoy their picnic in their field, each waving their arms with excitement. It is a time to discuss the surrounding area and their upcoming crops. There is the emotion of being home.

Jean later followed with his seriousness: "I can now work hard for God and King."

BATTLE

Jean was often dressed in non-fashionable attire, influenced by Aboriginal garb. His community had now manufactured his leathers, including moccasins and leather leggings.

Almost five years have transpired since their arrival. Jean worked both on carpenter focused projects with his father, and on their farm, but he wanted to broaden his experiences in life. Jean knows that his parents want change, but he needed to make a presentation. They would want the facts. They sat around the dinner table with candles dimly lighting the room.

He began his explanation to both parents patiently: "The Jesuits have promised to pay our family one hundred francs for the first year of my service. It is before August when I'll be nineteen years old. My term starts then and I'll continue to give service to the Jesuit missionary cause for one year."

Jean was also thinking that he now would not be banished from their community for not being married. He would be past the allowable age, but he was waiting for something that he did not understand. Perhaps love?

His mother brought him back to reality.

Michèle asks: "They are also building a college, are they not?"

Jean explains further: "Yes. The Jesuit superior, Father Jean Lalemant, documents every achievement in detail. They call it the science of crafts - *la science des ouvrages* - and it's given along with a program of training in which many are able to learn to read." He hesitates knowing they might not be in agreement with the total concept of the college: "They also learn to, write, play the viola and even excel in other fine arts such as embroidery."

William asks; "It's just training for young ladies is it not?"

Jean answers: "Yes,usually, but the goal is twofold. The settlers' homes are to become fit habitations by the Jesuits perceived standards; and secondly their churches need embellishing. I'll be working there to help achieve some of those goals for the year."

Michèle smiles broadly with delight: "Community good is linked to spiritual salvation. That includes the Jesuits' fine arts programs. We have seen a lot of change - within only a few years."

Such was Jean's original intent for his involvement with the local Jesuits. It was very passive. One month later would prove that many things can remain the same with intent, but at the same time become dissimilar by actions.

Late in the month of August Jean and others left Trois-Rivières in a fleet of eighty canoes bound for *Sainte-Marie aux pays des Hurons* - a Jesuit outpost and a major fortress.

Jean is at the head of his canoe as he speaks to his fellow Canadian warrior: "It's a very important fortress. We have no choice but to go. With it being located on Georgian Bay, Lake Huron, its very survival may prove to be pivotal to our surviving here."

His canoe partner is not so sure: "I'm told that the compound includes the church, housing for the French settlers and Jesuit missionaries, workshops, warehouses and a small medical dispensary. But if we can't save it, it will be rebuilt, won't it?"

Jean ignored his question: "There are also lodges for visiting Hurons. We can develop friendships with the indians."

"All indians are not bad indians," was the typical response.

Jean is committed: "If you wonder how important I think it is, just be aware that I intend to stay with the Jesuits - at least for one year."

"That's commitment," is the response in agreement.

Jean continued: "We'll be a "Christian community for the conversion of the natives. As settlers we always share the Jesuit mission statement."

His second partner's name is Louis. He counters with: "It's a difficult time, it tests every individual's strength of character on all levels."

Jean says: "Iroquois battles have begun, but also this effectively puts an end to the French-Huron alliance."
Louis says: "Even so, one-half the Huron population of Georgian Bay has died from epidemics brought by the Jesuits and even by us as *coureurs des bois*."

They are all aware that the survival of their own community was dependent on the teaching of the Hurons and others. No group of Europeans could flourish as they had, without learning the basics of clothing, hunting, fishing and producing food from the Indian bands.

Jean becomes emotional: "When Champlain had visited Huronia, he counted thirty-thousand people living in eighteen small towns. They're now only a few thousand."

Louis and Jean were concentration mostly on leaning into the task of canoeing. They were making good time.

Jean finally looked up and added: "The Indians can be a problem. In 1642, right after we arrived, the Jesuit Isaac Jogues was captured and tortured by the Iroquois. He was finally released."

Jean paused again to lean into his ultimate task then continued: "He returned to living with the Indian bands three years later. He now had a knowledge of their culture and he committed himself to living among them. With a single axe stroke to his head, he was killed by one of the many unconverted. It was a bloody end to his attempt to create peace with the Iroquois."

They kept canoeing as if talking about the weather.

Jean tried not to be racist. "There are at least four Indian nations that are friendly, even cooperative in their dealings with us.

"But the Iroquois are a military force to be reckoned with. The twelve thousand members of the Five Nations can summon twenty-two- hundred disciplined warriors at a moment's notice," states Louis on a serious note.

Jean continues paddling, laying in with a force: "I know we are in trouble. One out of ten of our European based population has been killed in Iroquois raids."

Louis agrees: "Yeh, I know, it's dangerous to go hunting or fishing as we fear for our lives."

He paused to concentrate on his paddle stroke and then continued: "We no longer can focus on clearing the land. The expense of bringing horses or mules from France would be wasted; the Iroquois would kill them shortly after they arrived."

Jean had gained knowledge on what were then world affairs. It was difficult, as most often that knowledge was based on rumour or at best the facts were two years old: "France is no longer interested in giving military support - its engaged in a war with Spain. That's why the alliance with the Huron needs to lead to ties between us. But because of the hatred between the Iroquois and the Huron, the Iroquois will remain our enemy. This canoe fleet is our show of force."

Louis smiles as they had a common ground and he summarizes: "It's complicated."

He pauses and adds: "But I agree". They paddle for half of the day without incident, nearing their destination.

Joseph shouts from the port side canoe. Jean and Louis can't hear him the first time. He shouts again. The sound is muffled by the roar of the river.

Jean yells: "What's that?"

Louis said: "It didn't seem real, it was flying."

Joseph yells back: "That's not snow, my brothers! The Indians are shooting arrows from the north bank!"

Jean shouts: "Head for the south bank."

Louis yells: "That's a given!"

Joseph is pulling his canoe up onto the shore. He is being sarcastic when he shouts: "It's about our show of force."

"We have a number of muskets," shouted Jean, as he pulled his canoe along side.

Joseph is concerned: "Did we count them?"

"We have fifty four, with almost two hundred rifles," says Jean. The canoes are landing together, being pulled out of the water with the men taking cover behind trees. They shoot back sparingly, waiting for a plan of action.

Louis shouts: "We need to get a better position."

"We're actually close to the compound. We can make it through the trees to there," suggests Joseph.

Jean counters: "That's what they expect. Let's do something different."

Louis is emotional: "Like shoot back? We can't shoot through trees."

Jean states his plan: "If we go back downstream, they'll be surprised. We can ford the river and attack them from their rear. Remember the sand bars? They weren't too far back."

Louis says: "We all would have to be together on this."

Joseph declares: "Some of the men can stay here as a decoy, to create the surprise from the rear."

Jean looks around. The other men are arriving in a cluster and are looking to him for direction, as at nineteen he is one of the eldest.

Jean understands his position and he shouts: "Let's do it!" He begins to run back towards the sand bars. Follow me, guys. We're about to have the show of force that we came for."
Forty men stay with Joseph and the rest run with Jean through the trees and head downstream. Over one hundred and sixty men are about to surprise the Iroquois still on the river's edge. After crossing the river on the sand bar, they make their way as silently as possible to the height of the rocks above the north river bank. They are above the Iroquois.

Louis is the first to speak. "This is better than we could have imagined. We have them in an ambush against the river."

Jean cautions: "Wait until we're all here. We can shoot all at once."

The full force of men quickly join them and find adequate cover from the volley of arrows that they expect would soon appear. Louis whispers: "We're all ready."

Jean shouts: "Fire!" The Iroquois are surprised by the sound and volley of so many muskets being behind them. They head for the river. Some have canoes, while others grab hold onto the canoes of others from their side. With this some tip over. It is a hasty retreat and complete chaos.

Louis shouts with glee as they watch the fleeing Iroquois: "I'm glad they didn't count our numbers."

Jean shouts for all to hear: "They may be back soon. Let's pick up our canoes and head for the compound."

Louis is already headed out. He shouts back: "Let's go guys!"

As the group finally approaches the compound towards nightfall, all seems abnormally quiet. The eight-foot wall is only made up of poplar tree stakes and it seems very inadequate compared to what they had just witnessed. They shout to be allowed to enter a gate, then gather in front of the small church and the administrative building.

The Jesuit Priest walks out to address them. He makes presumptions about their battle and asks solemnly: "How many are killed?"

Jean replies: "None. We have three men wounded."

"Bring them into the building. There are beds there. We can help a little," the priest offers.

Jean looks around: "Can you use food or water? You don't seem to have much."

The priest says: "We haven't dared leave the compound for three weeks. We were about to starve."

Jean goes into action: "Let's ten of us split off and bring back meat. Moose or deer, even rabbit."

Louis follows with: "Five or so of us will catch fish from down river. There are nets here that we can use."

Jean says: "You'd better take more men than that. The Iroquois may be watching. You may have to fight and retreat back in a hurry." Louis turns and waves to a cluster of men to follow: "We're on it."

Jean turns to the priest: "Father, that'll leave enough men to protect the compound. I hope you feel safe now."

"Hungry, mostly."

Jean smiles knowingly: "We'll get right on it."

***

About three hours later at dusk, Jean and the other hunters are returning. Louis and his group have fished until dusk also. As they arrive near the compound both parties find that they are in the rear position of an Iroquois attack on the poorly fortified premises.

Louis, seeing Jean, points at the Iroquois who are slowly moving ahead and stalking the compound. They are moving up to the fence and obviously are about to pounce as a full force.

Jean whispers, just loud enough for his group: "Wait until we're closer." He motions: "Fan out."

Both the hunting and the fishing group wait until they are assembled.

Jean shouts: "Fire. Let them have it!"

Again, due to complete surprise, and not knowing the numbers of opponents, the Iroquois retreat to the side through the opening. Louis stated his amazement: "Again we're on God's side.."

"Fate is with us, that's all," says Jean, immediately wishing he hadn't debated the point.

They walk into the compound gate and the priest is delighted. He looks at the two deer and the hooks of fish being offered.

He looks at Jean and asks: "Are you, by chance, the young man sent to be a donne, giving your services to the Jesuit missionary cause?"

Jean says: "Yes, I'm Jean Pelletier. At your service."

The priest shows a sense of humour: "We appreciate your versatility, Jean."

In 1646 Jean stayed on, serving the outpost of *Sainte- Marie aux pays des Hurons* and was listed as a "donné" of the Jesuits, that is, he gave his services to this specific Jesuit missionary cause.

He had acted outside of his church duties to say the least. He had joined the most major counter assault against the Iroquois in his young countries history. Jean spent almost a full year at Sainte-Marie.

As a young man, both devout and willing to learn, Jean fit in well. The four seasons pass quickly. It was both a process of surviving hardships and also of learning skills, some of which are available from the college and some which are more specific to survival.

THE INTERVIEW
Jean Talon

The concept of a young habitant being called in to be interviewed by the first Intendant of New France, Jean Talon, is not out of the ordinary.

Monsieur Jean Talon is the most successful of the Intendants for the very reason that his focus is on the details of the business of rural agriculture, civilization and the concept of a peaceful lifestyle.

In 1647, Jean Pelletier had returned to Beauport and the comforts of his parent's home. He was ready to focus on both civilization and family.

Two issues were now changed. A meeting with the Intendant Jean Talon would now summarize his community involvement after his return.

Jean walks into the Intendant's office showing the respect due to the intimidation of the formal building. He makes sure that any mud is wiped off his boots and he takes off his jacket. As far as he knows he is carrying it properly.

Sitting behind a massive desk, Monsieur Talon was attired in a wig, a fact that seemed weird to his young observer. He was dressed in a brocade dressing gown with a lavishly trimmed shirt, sporting unique lace at the wrists.

He seemed to flaunt the fact that he had an elegant lace cravat; as he continuously fluffed it up with a quick brush of the hand. Jean thought him okay as a man, in spite of this unique garb - a type of dress rarely seen by a habitant.

Jean Pelletier was a farmer with clothing made from rough durable fabrics - wool, canvas or upon occasion when hunting, hides similar to aboriginal dress.

Today Jean wore a wide brimmed hat and knee breeches. His shirt was made of white cotton with a collar and buttoned cuffs. Jean's pants were fitted at the knee with knitted long wool stockings. Ties of canvas were tied at his neck with both ends falling over his chest. Their contrast in clothing seemed considerable, possibly to both of them.

It seems that Monsieur Talon got right to the point: "You're a leader in this new land." It was just a statement.

"No Sir". Jean was trying not to appear insolent by being contrary: "I'm a potter - an artist."

Monsieur Talon ignored his statement: "I would like you to be involved with my administration. I'm told that you can read and write. You would be useful in my service."

Jean knew he would decline. He knew that he was not of a mentality that could be as subservient, as would be required.

Monsieur Talon continued: "I am, of course, concerned with our new college and the science of our crafts. I believe that you have learned from this program, albeit, indirectly. That in itself is unique. What is it that you do now in our land, young man?"

Jean answers: "Like other craftsmen, I'm an artist." He knew he was repeating himself, seemingly with no choice.

"And what makes you an artist, young man."

Jean smiles, as he is comfortable with the answer. He knew that it could have been a much harder quiz: "The mere assemblage of boards or general material does not satisfy me. It seems also that from the poorest non-farm owning peasant, to the wealthiest seigneur, things of beauty are of importance. It is often written that good taste knows no social barrier, Sir."

"As Intendant I co-exist here with Bishop Laval. Even though he might seem to be a bit of a scoundrel, we share the philosophy of being devoted to pursuits in both of our schools of arts and that of the crafts."

Jean says: "I am happy to have served for the year, Sir. I took advantage of studies at the same time."

Monsieur Talon summarizes: "The subjects now include science, that being navigation and seamanship, sculpting, carving, paneling, carpentry and joinery, architecture, silversmith work and pottery."

Jean says: "I pursued the making of ceramics, Sir. I became known as a goblet maker."

Monsieur Talon states: "I know of your work."

Jean is amazed at the comment, but he carries on without hesitation: "I have now returned to Beauport."

Monsieur Talon sits back in his chair, in a fatherly manner: "Exquisite furniture, beautiful churches and ornate chapels are becoming a part of our community. You will do well."

Jean says: "Thank you, Sir. Being involved as one of a working force with the Jesuits was also an honour and one of faith for our family."

Monsieur Talon continues with his philosophy: "The isolation from France may prove to be a cultural disaster. The break is so complete that the heritage of our evolving school of design is doubtful. Tell me about your studies."

Jean answers: "French medieval potters glazed their pots by brushing them with powdered galena gum that they made themselves - which is highly poisonous. I think that many died due to alcoholic poisoning. It is a learned experience of knowing which rocks could be ground to make the desired substance."

Monsieur Talon interrupts: "What led you to this study?"

"My father WIlliam had learned the basic process from his father. In growing up in the large village and creative centre of Chartres, France, Grandfather René had observed imported pottery technique," Jean answers proudly.

"Go on. I find this interesting."

Jean said: "I refined this process with the incorporation of slip evolving from studies with the Jesuits. Kilns need no complex system and I've built a simple one at my home."

"You are a habitant? Monsieur Talon already knew the answer, but he just wanted to see if the man's pride was there. Jean is proud of being from a habitant family having a registered deed. He considers his claim to being a habitant as if it is his own.

But, Jean continues to present himself as a potter: "Yes, and I'll simply dig into the side of a hill giving insulation. That provides room for the ash to fall clear for the air to pass under the burning fuel."

Monsieur Talon says with affirmation: "Arts and craft are important to our community."

Jean is more than happy to share his craft: "When clay is heated, steam is driven off, leaving the clay rigid. The mature clay particles melt into one another. Red clay is common in our pottery, and the high concentration of iron oxide - as shown by its colour."

"That explains the colour." Monsieur Talon smiled as he was being condescending in letting Jean carry on with his detailed explanation. The details were not actually important to him.

Jean explained further: "It lowers the melting point of clay. I'll fire the grey clays to a darker and creamier colour. The natural colour is purposely caused by rotten vegetation and reused for high fired pottery. It's called *stoneware*, or even *earthenware*."

Monsieur Talon rocks back in his chair and does his fatherly thing again: "I know that pottery is a primitive craft. But you can use glaze, which will be used to create a waterproof coating - but generally confined to the insides of pots and goblets."

"Yes Sir."

"Your work has come to my attention because of the use of slip and that copper is added to provide a green colour. And you have also used iron for yellow. If they are rough and porous in texture, they're grit-tempered by the addition of quartz sand or ground shell."

Jean is now even more enthusiastic. Jean Talon has given him affirmation as a personality from *above* in the higher order of things - *almost from God*: "I'll continue to dig my own clay. I know how to purify, dry, condition and adjust it with the knack of breaking, twisting and kneading the blocks of clay."

The door opens and Monsieur Talon's assistant entered the room. As he crosses the floor he offers his hand for shaking: "So you're the *Gobloteux*? I saw your work. I was the one that showed it to Monsieur Jean Talon here."

"Thank you, Sir."

The assistant has removed his cloak, Jean noticed that it was made of a material as rugged as his own attire. It was made of thick, grey homespun wool, probably brought from France - now worn out completely.

The assistant continues: "Your work is unique. One method is that of throwing clay on a very primitive wheel; however, due to the size and shape of most cups or goblets, a wheel is not always necessary and I'm told that you don't use one."

Jean smiled having achieved attention by both of his superiors.

The assistant knows of his pride as it is obvious and showing: "With that, your finishing and decorating has unique thickness, shapes and textures, by way of your scoring, and carving actions."

"Yes, Sir, I use a slip, a creamy liquid formed by adding water to a slurry - which in turn is produced by steeping dry clay in water for the casting process," Jean explains further.

The assistant interrupts him with the overview of showing who's opinion really mattered: "This is not a decorative process normally used in New France. You are producing the exception. Slip coating nicely transforms the appearance of common red clay for aesthetic reasons. Are you also able to obtain white clay?"

Jean adds for clarity: "Yes I often travel long distances."

The assistant reasserts his authority: "What is your intention?"

Jean replied: "I wish to sell my wares outside of my own district, even in the town of Quebec. They need not simply be serving daily domestic uses: the bowls, dishes, jugs, candlesticks and jars. I wish to make special pieces in honour of special events and decorate them."

Monsieur Jean Talon stands, as if to show it is his turn to be the authority. He states as a decree: "You shall be known by your art and craft. Both as a potter and as a designer you will be well known, as *Le Gobloteux* (the potter)."

"Thank you Sir."

The assistant enthusiastic, having the safety of his superior's response says: "Your unglazed earthenware bowls have their interior decorated with lines, circles or spots of brown slip, all over a white base slip. Many have a greenish over-glaze. You're doing much more than just goblets for beer and wine are you not?"

Jean answers politely: "When earthenware is intended for religious purposes it can be more ambitious."

Monsieur Talon is still in charge: "This year I will begin to build the first beer brewery. The enterprise is for three purposes: to promote temperance by offering an alternative to strong French liquors; to reduce the amount of currency leaving; and to utilize the abundance of grain available here."

He then summarizes their discussion to indicate that Jean's interview was over: "We are happy to have you as a part of our community, young *Gobloteux*. We can use your craft."

Jean leaves the rather formal meeting as politely as he has entered. He backs up almost to the door, turning only when he is about to exit. He adds the extra measure of putting on his coat later, when outside in the rather cold late afternoon air. Coincidently, it is all in the mannerism of being in a French court.

THE KING'S GIRLS

Jean walks to the house slowly after his long day in the field. He then washes with creek water from a wooden bucket, which is always left on a bench, just outside the cabin door. The water seems colder than usual, but it gives a jolt to his senses, separating his day of labour from his evening relaxation.

He had wished to discuss a forthcoming issue, but he had held off. Jean could not know what his parents' reaction would be. He would wait until after they ate. A meal prepared by his mother was always a reminder of what was good about this new land.

As evening arrives, the table, rugged and hand built, is cleared. The candles are lit - and Jean clears his throat. He begins: "I probably have no choice in something I want to discuss, but I need you to know my opinion."

His mother and father accept this as being an important subject. They give Jean their undivided attention.

"I needn't take the chance of marrying one of the imported group, the girls of unknown origin. They may be called "The King's Girls", ("les Filles du Roy") but of royalty they often are not," Jean was comfortable showing his prejudice.

WIlliam explains the rumour to his good wife in what seemed to be a condescending manner, presuming that she had not heard: "Our Intendant, Jean Talon, is going to issue an ordinance compelling bachelors to marry the King's Girls within 15 days of the arrival of the vessels bringing in the women, or they will be further prohibited from fishing, hunting and trading for furs."

Jean adds: "that applies to all men over nineteen."

Michèle replies: "I know. There will be hundreds of the girls sent out from France. Some may be very nice. They'll be here to provide the unmarried men with wives just as is needed."

She is hoping that her son would soon be married as it is far past time, not just legally but by her own expectations.

William provides his insight: "Many are poor but the king is providing them with a small dowry. Most are about fourteen years old. Not much older than Anne Langlois, who we know."

Jean waits his turn. He is always polite in these circumstances: "Upon their arrival at the docks in the harbour, they're to be paraded about on the wharf for the taking. The unmarried men are to quickly choose a fiancée from the chaos."

He pauses as if to allow the image of chaos to set in: "Girls are permitted to turn down a suitor, but they're not going to be too choosy. They need food and shelter."

Michèle consoles him: "They'll have accepted their fate and a meagre future in the colony. They're also aware that once married they are expected to be subject to discipline with the new rules. I've been told that a separation could only be obtained if their husband resorts to beating them with a stick thicker than their wrist. They will be obedient, Jean. That can be good, can it not?"

"But each couple is to be given an ox and a cow, two pigs, a pair of chickens, two barrels of salted meat and eleven crowns - a good start in life," interjected WIlliam - feeling that he had provided a very logical business approach.

Michèle has heard rumours about the positives for the community: "The King's Girls can produce literally hundreds of births per year."

Jean states his belief adamantly: "The births will be listed in documents, not unlike the production of wheat or the husbandry of cattle. The administration then is able to calculate their success. But it's too much like the flip of a coin!"

William doesn't understand the dilemma. He counters: "It solves the problem of the population being two-thirds male - even if husbandry is a logical study to both animals and settlers."

Jean smiles. This was his chance: "Anne Langlois, the girl almost next door, is my answer. She is only ten, but she is beautiful, worthy and strong. As habitants, we are free to marry at the church in Quebec City. The marriage contract can be signed at Robert Giffard's manor house.

Michèle stays in the conversation: "The manor house is the centre of life at the seigneury of Beauport."

It seems that neither parent had considered the obvious. They slowly change their almost business like manner in posture. They all relax and their facial expressions break into a smile.

William is overjoyed: "By having published your banns of marriage in the church, before you are officially announced as being over twenty, you'll have succeeded in abiding by the King's Rules. You also gain a pretty bride in the bargain. You even may gain the bounty called *The King's Gift* after your marriage within your stipulated age."

Jean puts his head on his folded arms on the table, with a huge sigh of relief. He yells: "Great! I am spared!" He is also thinking of a pretty young girl - Anne Langlois, soon to be a beautiful woman.

THE PROPOSAL

Two men casually meet in the wheat field. William, Jean's father, had made the visit and had addressed Anne's father, Noel, with the usual introductions and small talk. This meeting though, was intentional, planned by WIlliam.

As could be expected William now spoke formally as a man from his personal past. Expected because he knew no other way of speaking in such an uncomfortable situation. His speech was very much an imitation of his own father, Eloi - as he had remembered him in France.

William became serious and then abruptly stated his proposition: "The Garniers, your maternal family, are our neighbours here at Beauport and that is good. Their next door neighbors up from the falls, are you the Langlois."

William was projecting a soft voice for the occasion: "We know your mother Françoise Grenier well – a lovely woman." It was also a preamble to the idea that Anne, the granddaughter would be of the same character.

William continues as if in complete control: "We are suggesting that your lovely daughter Anne and our son Jean should be married. The wedding won't take place for another two years after the published bans, as Anne is only ten years old and the church won't allow the marriage of anyone under the age of twelve."

Anne's father, Noel Langlois, was not in disagreement. He seemed to be considering the idea out-loud: "Most marriages are held in November to February, the idle months of the year. It is between the hard labour of autumn and spring." Noel still held the air of a helmsman with somewhat having control of the sea.

William says: "Weddings are one of the main social events. The celebrations should last several days or even weeks. Should you agree, this Pelletier and Langlois wedding won't be an exception."

The necessary reply follows: "I look forward to it. Anne will be told."

It was a done deal. The two men would probably never be this formal in conversation again.

ANNE'S ENGAGEMENT

At ten years old and being told that she was engaged to be married, Anne's life changed. Some of the wonderment of childhood had to be set aside. She did understand that this was a mental commitment, but she believed that it would not change anything: "I can still relish the beauty of a butterfly. I'm still excited about flowers in the spring and cute birds chirping."

When she was told of her groom-to-be she wasn't shocked. She had no reason to react in any specific way. In July of 1647, life did unfold in a normal manner.

Her childhood could still be enjoyed, but other thoughts evolved. Being engaged, she discussed different facts with her two older sisters: "Working in the fields has been my only experience in anything that can resemble womanhood."

Marie, two years older, simply asked why she was worried.

"What do I know now about being a woman?"

Marie was specific: "Like all women, you can carry baskets of animal dung to help manure the fields. It's not fun, but it will never change."

Anne smiled: But I can look after the animals of the family kept around the house - the hens, pigs and cattle." She hadn't contemplated that in her future she wouldn't be living with her family.

Anne also would become worldly as a woman by new standards, and she knew it. Michelle, five years her senior, had told her of the changes in female virtues that she had heard from afar and Anne could consider the possibilities for her own life. Even morals would change.

Anne's window on the world was small and it actually was a window. Next to the wash basin, next to the kitchen shelves, she often would gaze on the meadow below.

The cabin was on an incline, just enough to produce a healthy run-off from spring thaws. Her view at the window, onto the meadow below was combined with housework.

She was surprised though, as normally an engagement would be at least another two years when she was older. But surprise could be replaced by becoming prepared and Anne was not indignant as she felt a sense of calmness - she was sure of herself. Her window on life was about to broaden as she now viewed the beauty of autumn leaves.

She felt sad that she needed to be married at twelve years of age but *that was the end of it*. There would be no questioning allowed on her part. Both of her older sisters agreed that her engagement followed a normal course of life. They had already been promised. They were both content with their arrangements. Her younger sister, Etiennet, was living more in a world of fantasy, and believed it was romantic and perfect in every way.

Anne wasn't sure what the pleasures of marriage were. She had heard about happiness with the joy of being a couple. A few women had mentioned it. Possibly it was a trade-off for hard labour, She didn't quite understand it.

Anne again thought about the two years grace until she turned twelve: "Surely I'll be more aware by then – I'm just a girl."

Noel had taken thin animal hides, shaved them as much as possible and soaked them in oil. This was called parchment. When Anne was older, window glass would become increasingly common, at least in the homes of the rich.

But now the windows were simply a small opening to let some light in - a hole in the wall covered by the thin hides. They held out the storms.

On Anne's window, as she thought of it, wooden shutters were used. Not just light was allowed in, but when the shutters were folded open and the weather allowed it, the beauty of her outdoor world was totally exposed. When closed shutters protected her from the cold winter and she was warm and safe. She felt that the inconsistent seasonal view was a symbol of the control the church held over her. It was sporadic, irregular and illogical. She enjoyed thinking such complicated things.

Anne had met Jean briefly when he had last visited to borrow some kind of tool. She had smiled at him, and he at her. "It wasn't romance," she thought.

She spoke to her sister Michelle about the meeting: "I was just a kid being friendly to a full-grown man."

Michelle was able to read and with that came a learned vocabulary: "Trust will have to follow admiration for Jean - his profile in the community and his appearance as a man. Admiration will win out."

Anne somehow thought about her fear, even of sex: "Acceptance is weaker than trust."

Anne knew that the population was young. A lot of men were about twenty - or even an old twenty-two if living outside the community. The women were all about fourteen. It had not occurred to Anne while she contemplated becoming a mother that only a few women embarked on a journey from France after the age of fourteen or fifteen. Most arrived before.

They were a *country of teenagers* and it was common for men to marry later than women. This was logical as men needed to become more financially capable in some manner. Whether that meant acquiring experience on their family farm or actually acquiring a registered habitation, it created a gap of four or five years for most couples.

In the case of the King's Girls the age gap would always be the most pronounced. Anne could only presume, as most believed – that those in charge of such things were wise, considerate and looking out for everyone's best interest.

Church and state combined were the ultimate rulers, not to be ignored in any way. In spite of Anne's obedience to her masters, as she perceived the administration and the church to be, she did wonder about unmarried life. Men enjoyed a life devoid of married drudgery and toil for many years, whereas women were to commit themselves to marriage and consistent birthing almost as children.

Anne's window of spring drew her outdoors. The opening of the shutters produced a necessity for rejoicing in a flowering landscape. The spell of cabin-fever was replaced by an abundance of life, singing birds and new births of spring's creation. She was drawn outside like never before, wanting no more of incarceration.

She was able to walk in the fields while in contemplation once more. She questioned Marie: "Is it true that it was written in the bible that women should be immediately put into servitude upon their first period?"

Marie was a loyal believer: "You need to simply believe it. And that's what the priest said."

In her quiet moments alone, she often sighed at the thought of a life never being different. It also seemed to Anne that the church only controlled adult minds. It seemed that it was only her childlike fantasies that allowed her to question the church's pronouncements. The church was surely correct.

The two years that Anne knew existed before she could actually be married seemed like an eternity to her ten-year old mind, but she was determined not to make a total commitment to the church until necessary.

She needed to make her position known to Marie: "I will wait until old age to receive the sacrament of confirmation. I have learned that it is possible to wait."

She smiled at having rebellious thoughts, Marie just ignored her.

Anne's thoughts were repetitious: "I'm sure that I'll gain the feeling of being a woman in that time – surely". She vowed to herself that she would spend the next two years still playing childhood games.

She was wrong and she spent the time learning household skills. She was about to leave her lighter duties of cleaning food preparation and mending. In general she would learn that woman's work was almost all of the hard labour. Anne also focused on creating a new garden as a source of vegetables.

Her shuttered window became even larger with romantic thoughts. She was gaining mature thought and the mentality of an older person compared to her chronological age. Anne smiled at the romantic prospect of making an adult home in their candlelit cottage. She trusted that her confusion would vanish and that womanhood would take over in some miraculous way.

However, Anne's last thoughts each night as she fell asleep were questions of what might be necessary in becoming a woman. She thought that mentally coping and physically surviving was sometimes the same thing.

The three banns of marriage (proclamations) were published during three feast days in June. The congregation was told over three consecutive Sundays that Anne and Jean were to be wed . As was necessary, the banns were well planned ahead of time.

However it was rumoured as a disgrace that when time arrived for the wedding ceremony, someone had discovered a canonical reason to stop the wedding, It was related to the banns of marriage being incorrectly published. At the engagement Anne Langlois was not ten years old since she was born on September 2 1637. With this stoppage evolving from the rumour, the actual wedding had to be postponed until she was of age, which was 12 years old.

Anne could now gaze out her window for three of the four seasons, vibrant in the green colours of spring finally turning to the warmth of summer and the vivid colours of fall. It was as a young woman standing looking outward on life.

Her engagement announcement was formal and Anne felt that it had a wonderful sound to it. She was engaged to: *"Jean Pelletier-dit-Gobloteur", born June 12, 1627 in St. Aubin de Tourouvre, Mortagne Orne, Perche Region, France.* She repeated it to herself four times outloud and smiled.

Anne's new life meant that along with dealing with puberty, a change in her body, she had to deal with the constant evolution of her new adult mind. She had to speculate what it would mean to her new husband. She would be moving away from her window in the small cabin, to a life with Jean.

As a little girl, Anne had continued wearing a bigger version of a nursery gown until she left France. Now it was a given that her little girl world would be set aside. In leaving France, her treasured doll was her greatest loss, in this painful process of having to *grow-up*.

She would now don a waist length and sleeveless corset bodice over her chemise (a knee length undergarment) that could function as a blouse, common among the poor. Over the corset, she wore a waistcoat, fitted and made of heavy wool. Beneath the corset bodice and waistcoat, she wore one or more petticoats (skirts) and stockings held up by garters above the knee, both providing warmth in cold weather.

She would normally wear an apron, typically made of dark plain linen. This might be nothing more than a piece of cloth tucked into the waistband of her skirt - maybe with the upper piece of it pinned to her bodice. To top off her ensemble, she wore a felt hat over a linen *coif,* which was a cap that fit over her pinned-back blond hair.

Anne often wished that she could wear a linen collar, it would not even be necessary for it to be trimmed in lace -not trimmed like the rich.

Anne did not entirely question authority by the church and ultimately the king. The dictated idea of a set of rules for dress, was only philosophical, but it needed to be practical. She would make her own clothes, which were expected by all of the rules to resemble attire seen in rural France. In those rules, she failed.

Here, woolen under clothes were worn all year round - in winter for warmth and in summer to absorb perspiration. Anne even wore added skirts for warmth.

To survive the cold winter, habitant women sometimes copied the First Nations clothing - mitten and moose leather boots lined with beaver fur and fur lined coats and moccasin type footwear for warmer seasons. This was a deviation far away from the style of rural France and the cold wooden clogs that Anne hated. She loved her moccasins.

Women wore small caps or nets covering their close curls and the long hair gathered into a bun in the back. A woman rarely had her hair completely uncovered, and an older or widowed woman would likely be even more covered. Anne often wore a kerchief called a head cloth. She braided her hair wrapping it circularly around the back. She could then cover the braids with a small cap or cloth that was often woven into the braids.

The work of ploughing was left to her father and her brothers, but she was to help gather the harvest. Gleaning and picking up grains of corn the male harvesters had left behind was commonly the younger women's task, those not yet married. Anne worked hard at it for two harvests until her wedding.

Her youthful time was now spent logically, learning her duties well, both in the field and within the cabin.

She was sure that Jean would trap animals easily and that they could be skinned, with pelts used to line winter clothes. In this, she knew that she would be expected to help and she didn't think of it as negative by any means. Warmth would be provided.

By Anne's perception Jean would express kindness and not cruelty - there would be no suffering and weeping. As the two years went by, she lived her more mature life in high spirits.

Fortunately she was able to spend some time with Jean now that they were promised to each other. She would attend functions knowing that he was there.

They would meet, steal time together and romantically enjoy a walk in the moonlit night. The moon would reflect off the snow in a white-blue haze, providing an evening for young couples to be enthralled. Friendship would develop as a band of joy between them, as they came together and had fun. It became the tender feeling of love.

LOUIS

On what seemed to be the other side of the world, it is in the French Court where a Court Reader formally reads a document sent from Jean Talon. He is the intendant of the new part of the French speaking earth. The reader speaks loudly: "As for the business matters in New France, and further to any rumours about the insolence shown to France on the part of those in the colony, I have this news. Our most successful Intendant, Jean Talon communicated the following My Lords."

"One must not expect to make people here submissive and always respectful of the King's law and of those who represent his authority, since there has probably never been a country where so many people, even the foremost in every profession, have sought to deny it."

The group made sounds of disagreement.

The Court Reader continued: "For the first time, under my direction, the administration of New France will be focused on rural agricultural realities and peaceful lifestyles. I am now known as Jean Talon the businessman, within the ultimate industry of agriculture. I am not a Military General, nor do I intend to pursue any military gains." Having finished the quote the Reader bowed to his superiors and sat down.

After much informal bickering within the group, a member of the court stood and addressed his colleagues: "I would like to draw attention to the fact that the projections of Jean Talon do consistently include his people's husbandry schemes. The very most important of which, includes the *King's Girls* shipments. His popularity may always be that in all of this, he is very straightforward and never devious in admitting his intent in such matters."

They talk among themselves, none making any sense and none considering the actual overall good of the land they are becoming to know as Canada. It was simply a decision about an impersonal investment, that of the cost of creating a business return from a place far away.

***

The Court Reader had described Louis. From an unfathomable distance away the members of government were hearing that: "One must not expect to make people here submissive and always respectful of the King's law and of those who represent his authority, since there has probably never been a country where so many people have sought to deny it."

Louis chose to be a toiler of the land, but his motivation was not to please "God and King". He felt he had arrived in Canada free from the tyranny of France. He would attempt to be self-sufficient for his entire adult life.

As a great consequence, he failed to marry at the proper age of nineteen. He would now accept his banishment from his own community and become a man of the great wilderness.

***

Until his being condemned to the forests he wore a shift or shirt, breeches with knitted wool stockings, and sometimes a vest or a short waistcoat. He would not experience the elite leather shoes with a buckle and until he left his community he wore clogs.

Aboriginal influence from around the great lakes to the east gave him the benefit of moccasins. In addition to them, he added leggings and on super humid days, breechclouts (a rectangular piece of fabric held up by a belt). A toque or a wide brimmed hat was normally worn depending on the season.

Being ready for whatever the wilderness offered, he could now hire himself out as a *coureur des bois;* as he and others now travelled as far west as the series of upper waterways of the Great Lakes *(the "pays d'en haut").* Louis would now spend months at a time living among the natives. Traditionally, the government of New France preferred to let the natives supply furs directly to French merchants, and discouraged French settlers from venturing outside the Saint Lawrence valley.

But, in the mid-sixteen hundreds, Louis like others, would be of a mind that resulted in a sudden spike in the number of coureurs des bois. First, the population of New France markedly increased as the colony experienced a boom in immigration. Many chose freedom in the life of the coureur des bois away from French restrictions.

Also becoming a coureur des bois became both more feasible and profitable. Louis along with his friends would often use goods as currency in exchange for the furs to be transported.

PAUL

The artist was David Teniers the Younger.
The painting is titled "Summer", painted in 1660.

Paul was initially a silent man, withdrawn by most standards. But in his teenage years he had joined in with the enjoyable rebellion of Louis and Joseph. They had shown their objection to French rules involving hierarchy and dress codes, as the three young men each wore a cloak (*Quebec capot*). They would march around the settlement, showing up at festivals, sporting the homespun garment. They had intended to make a statement about freedom from France. But even looking dashing in their demeanor, they were actually laughed at by many of the more practical in their community.

In France, embroidered woollen cloth and furs were the clothes worn by the rich. To dress differently meant that it would be misleading and cloaks were not acceptable for them. That list was taken from one of a 1597 French Proclamations against *excess of apparel* strictly controlled in minute detail.

Only earls could wear silk cloth. No one under the degree of knight was allowed silk long stockings or velvet outer garments. A knight's eldest son could wear velvet doublets and hose, but his younger brothers couldn't. A baron's eldest son's wife could wear lace, forbidden to women below her in the pecking order.

But none of this had an effect on the *New World* order. The wearing of a cloak by Paul, Louis and Joseph was significant by flaunting an idea that was political. They felt free.

* * *

The *King's Rules* are specific, with the age of marriage being ordered. Paul's father had failed to have his son married by twenty. Paul knew he and his father would be hauled into the court every six months until a mate could be found. He then wouldn't be allowed to fish, hunt or trap in even a nearby community.

Paul preferred the life of a habitant. This represented being allowed to toil and harvest within a stable system. For a few years Paul aided his father on his farm. But then he turned twenty and it was time to move on.

He would not travel west until the birthday. It was during the farming years that he received visits from his older *courier des bois* friends. They would attend Anne and Jean's wedding in their usual frolicking way - a bit drunk for the occasion. He later joined them for the adventure of canoeing over vast terrain.

Paul's oppressed nature changed in the wild. As a courier des bois he observed the aggressiveness of others and gained confidence. After a stint in the boot camp of the wilderness he was ready to return to farming and as was expected he took a wife within a short time upon returning.

Paul was as part of the wedding party. Being a bit younger than Jean and stouter, he was to be an aid whenever the work of the farm was too difficult - whenever heavy lifting was needed. On the north shore of the Saint Lawrence river, he was known for his strength and his willingness to help his neighbours. All farmers need a friend like Paul.

JOSEPH

Joseph had been taught that an ideal medieval gentleman had many virtues. The rules had often been explained by his grandfather. Through the hierarchy in which his ancestors existed, he was to be loyal to his feudal obligations and conscientious in the administration of justice. He was to be generous, particularly in bequeathing money to the church. He was sincerely religious, respectful of church and authority, and faithful to his duties in these. He seldom violated an oath or solemn promise, believing that these were recorded in heaven and breaching them would be divinely punished as perjury. Above all, he was never disobedient.

He had rebelled and this was not the mindset of Joseph, with any contemplation of the medieval or otherwise.

The antique medieval society of France was sharply stratified with social gradations. This carried onto the time of the community that included Louis, Joseph, Paul, Anne and Jean. Before living in the new world everyone believed in the doctrine of nobility by birth.

The community had nuances to which all classes conformed without question. Status affected the seats in church, and in their position on a Saint's Day; class lines were formalized with distinct styles of dress, diet, habitation and entertainment, each having its own training, customs and mental attitudes. Hierarchy was considered a very positive measure of civilization. The belief was that social hierarchy preserved political and economic order. To believe in the equality of human beings was to be uncivilized.

As a colonist, Joseph would be the first of his family to accept living and working without the medieval social concepts.

**

It is any river shore, anywhere in the area of the waterways leading to the Great Lakes. A group of canoes have been brought up to the river's bank, they are secured, and a number of men are assembling and making camp.

Dressed much like their aboriginal friends many of this group will explore, perish, become legendary or perhaps become nameless. They are Jean and Anne's friends, Joseph, Louis and Paul. It is a favourite type of conversation.

Paul shouts out: "We enjoy this! We are called the brash young men of our village, we who were unwilling to be told what we may or may not do."

Joseph agrees: "We left under very strict rules. It's no wonder we leave all of that in great numbers."

Louis is more specific: "Jean Talon called us bandits and church decrees make us outlaws. Yet we open up the wilderness interior and we enlarge the fur trade."

"Our exodus from the small eastern villages is so great that the loss of the males in Quebec is said to be one-quarter of the male population," said Paul.

Louis says: "The habitants had learned to use the cold to preserve food, and their homes withstood frost and thaws. Their clothes were warm and they learned to adapt to travel on snowshoes. But now we can learn even more from our Indian friends. Here we can conquer all the wilds of this land."

Louis adds: "We are taxed for as long as we remain unmarried. That's what happened to me!"

Paul still shouts: "It's a time of restrictions on everything. But I'm now a free man!"

They laugh together as a shared joke. But they also had shared their loneliness in this vast land. They continue to set up camp. There is a brief pause in the list of daunting issues. Then it begins anew. These men are both relieved and frustrated to have left their homes and family.

.

Louis said: "We have heard stories about the five Great Lakes and we have decided to explore them."

Paul shares his enthusiasm: "We'll set off from Lake Couchiching and through the Narrows to Lake Simcoe."

Joseph agreed: "Then we can travel along the portage route called the Toronto Carrying Place – a trail along the Humber River and down to Lake Ontario."

Paul laughed: "Because the river is full of rapids and it'll snake back and forth for a great part of its route. We'll overcome even that. We'll carry our canoes."

They agreed.

Paul continued: "It'll be easier to carry birchbark canoes and supplies even through the thick forest - than to paddle along the river and we can reach most posts within a month of paddling - even if we have a few dozen portages!"

Louis was always practical: "I'm glad they're made of light birchbark. We also learned that from the indians."

Joseph added to the excitement, this was the freedom he enjoyed: "We can get our food as we travel - even sleep under whatever shelter can be found in the great forests!"

Louis added: "We'll go up the Ottawa River. Our route is formed by lakes, small rivers, rapids and waterfalls. We'll take the Abitibi River to reach the Hudson Bay."

Joseph also knew his geography: "And then to reach the great lakes, we turn left at the Mattawa fork, and then take the small river, crossing Lake Nipissing."

Louis shared information, often repetitious, but welcome among the group: "And later the Riviere des Francais to reach the junction of Lake Huron and Lake Michigan!"

**

Joseph fit the profile of an ideal courier des bois. He was rugged, preferring an almost savage lifestyle and looking for love within another culture to the west. He was described as unshaven, with long straight hair and being tall he tended to hunch over others in a Neanderthal fashion.

Joseph searched for the enjoyment and quietness of nature. He relished being in the woods and later in life, he would enjoy his time on the wide expanse of the prairies. Big blue sky, small winding creeks, snow on the forest - all were his home.

He was a free person who abandoned his European culture in search of a better life. But the independent *coureur des bois* was gradually replaced by sponsored *voyageurs* who were workers associated with government licensed fur traders. Joseph was not to be taken in by this more structured life. He was not available to work for someone else.

After initially leaving, Joseph returned to the settlements of the St. Lawrence river valley only twice in his lifetime. He trapped and hunted on his own terms.

The Adventures of Paul, Joseph and Louis: "Shooting The Rapids" by Arthur Heming

Paul, Joseph and Louis in later years.

THE WEDDING

The community was initiated by a country of teenagers.

Jean married Anne Langlois on November 9th, 1649 in the Chapel of Seigneur Giffard, Québec City. She was stated as being the daughter of Noel Langlois in a time when female names were without identity. She now had an identity as being the wife of *Jean Pelletier-dit-Gobloteur* (The goblet maker's wife).

On November 9, 1649, at Beauport, Father Jean LeSueur blesses the wedding ceremony, which took place at Beauport. Jean, age 22, and Anne, age 12 were finally wed. That the ceremony was in Seigneur Giffard's home and personal chapel was not unusual. The habitants, by their actual definition, owed allegiance to their Seigneur, as chattels; to wed, give birth and be buried under his rules.

Other than ignoring a notarization by the priest, all is perfect. "He may have not forgiven Anne for holding back on her total commitment to the church;" was her thought.

Mostly Anne was concerned with her dress. Her sisters had told her that it should be blue. Woad as a dye had been used in France and they were now using it in the New World. Dyer's woad, of the mustard family, bloomed in early summer. The dye extracted from woad is called indigo. The dying process went well and Anne knew that she could wear her skirt with pride in the future.

She wore a waist length and sleeveless corset bodice, functioning as a blouse, over her undergarments. Over the corset, she wore a dyed blue wool waistcoat. She wore three petticoats and stockings held up by garters. Anne was overjoyed at being able to wear a linen collar. It was trimmed in lace and was special for the occasion.

Her two older sisters had worn the lace collar at their weddings. Other women had also worn it in years prior. No one would doubt the logic of enjoying the beauty of a lace collared dress - no matter if it had become more beige than white.

Anne had vowed to Etiennet: "I will share this beautiful collar with you when the time comes."

"I'm just a child," replied Etiennet.

Anne thought about her own fears and her wish to remain a child only a few years ago.

To top off her ensemble, Anne wore a felt hat over a linen cap that fit over her blond hair. Being young she had no confidence in her ensemble, but knew that Jean loved her smile. She reminded herself that he had actually stated that.

It is a beautiful day in a wonderful setting of green rolling hills covered with trees of pine and spruce. A slight covering of snow adds to the beauty, giving the scene a winter wonderland look. As if to accent the perfection, the sky is a clear blue showing a blessing from that which each individual considers to be from *on high*.

The reception is in the large room of Seigneur Giffard's grandiose manor home after the wedding in the chapel. The neighbours are all in attendance dressed in their best. If they only owned one set of clothes, they were washed and ready.

Due to William's involvement in local politics, the union is in the presence of Jean Juchereau, Sieur de La'Ferte, Jean Guyon and Jean Cote, presenting a personal authorization, all important individuals, but mostly in their own minds.

Anne's sisters attended to her needs, which were almost non-existent. At the wedding ceremony they stood proudly on her left. Louis, Joseph and Paul stood informally on Jean's right.

Louis, Joseph and Paul had returned from adventures in the wild. After the ceremony and with a mug of beer in hand, Paul stated with enthusiasm: "Apparently, they have registered their marriage at Quebec City? Not all marriages are documented."

Joseph also looked forward to imbibing. He says: "No, but that was in June and July, two years ago, the banns of marriage were some kind of mistake and they were incorrectly published."

Joseph is handed a goblet of beer by Paul, who says: "It was announced three times at Quebec and it was very formal, but not here locally. They had it redone." He sometimes wanted to sound as if he was interested in church legalities. He wasn't.

Louis counters with: "The reality was that the parents were also convinced that for Anne this marriage was ideal. They may have not announced locally for a reason - maybe Jean's age. He was over."

"Jean wasn't averse to the choice. He's twenty-two now. She was a pretty young girl; he could only believe that she would become a beautiful young woman," said Joseph.

Paul says: "On the other hand Anne had no choice. Love can come later."

"I noticed that they wed without a notarized marriage contract. Am I right about that?" Louis is more curious than anything. He knew that there was no reason that his friends would be concerned, or even knowledgeable.

Paul refers to the other possible problem and attempted to make a joke about it: "Although Anne's age is ideal, Jean is over age by at least two years. He is over the hill my friends."

Paul paused for effect and raises his glass: "God be with him."

It is a shared laughter as they are all about the same age. Jean sees them laughing and he takes Anne by the hand and joins them.

Paul is caught off guard. Thinking that he might have said something wrong for the occasion, he catches himself quickly with a response: "Congratulations, of course. You are both beautiful and handsome today."

Joseph smiles widely: "Congratulations, and we will be seeing you both around - with your new growing family? As it comes of course."

He has another swig of his drink: "When do you move into the Langlois home?"

Jean explains: "We will do the opposite and move in with my parents rather than with the bride's family. It's unusual, but, what's unusual for these times? The Langlois house is home to eight children. Our Pelletier homestead on the other hand, will only have us - and my parents."

Anne is happy in her new role and she is showing off to their friends. She turns obediently to Jean. They observe a hint of womanhood within her subservience: "Will we live here forever, Jean? Land is being settled in all of the St. Lawrence Valley. You said that in the summer we'll use a canoe or sailing barque and in winter a sleigh on the river ice."

Jean is authoritative, but with a smile: "Not forever. Farming is not forever. My art and craft is alive also." He could now flaunt his leadership within his family.

Anne wants to seem very adult today, showing a positive future and intellect, in spite of her little-girl charm: "At the June processions of the Fête du Saint Sacrement, representatives will march carrying a torch. They'll be like their guild in Old France."

Jean falls into step and shows himself as being her partner: "Three years ago there was a carpenter, mason, toolmaker, baker, brewer and sailor. Now there also is a joiner, turner, locksmith, gunsmith, shoemaker, cooper, wheel-right and nail-maker."

Anne smiled, quite proud of herself: "We hold a common birthplace - the province of Perche in France. I know well the names of Aubin, Baril, Beaulac, Bouchard, Boucher, Cloutier, Drouin, Gagnon, Giguère, Lambert, Landry, Leduc, Lefèbvre, Mercier, Rivard and Tremblay. We'll live here as a well-founded community."

They had made their speeches, Jean made his as a new community leader and Anne as a new adult member. It was their day to be listened to and it would continue to be that way for the duration of the wedding celebration.

All the guests respected Anne and welcomed her into her new adult status. The seemingly important men of their community gave their blessings.

As usual Paul, Joseph and Louis all had fun. But they had seen a change in this community gathering. The three men had both observed and had listened to their former neighbours about the new rules.

They were enjoying the produce of Monsieur Jean Talon's new beer brewery. After a few drinks they needed to vent their frustration. They are sitting to the side of this church and community hall, observing the young ladies dancing.

Louis speaks out: "Here's one for you! I've heard that women have to be home by nine."

"Unmarried girls are permitted to dance only with one another, in their homes, or with their mothers always present," says Joseph.

Paul adds: "There'll be no dancing for us tonight! Even as we are liking the music. I like good fiddle music."

Louis observes: "Rouge is also now forbidden even for older women. It wasn't before."

Joseph states a different approach: "Hey, I've heard that even public meetings to discuss politics are not going to be allowed - for everyone."

"My God! And the punishment for profanity is harsh: a man's lips can be seared with a red-hot iron," Paul is also ranting.

"Creativity in using swear words will be the order of the day," laughs Joseph. "But we'll make a new vocabulary."

Paul summarizes: "But we can stamp our feet and watch the women dance - and listen to the fiddle music."

Joseph said: "The beer is good!"

But they had not forgotten the comparison to other regions of France. Life was good here, by all accounts.

* * *

Anne and Jean returned to the Pelletier cabin as a couple - somewhat changed. Jean with his new responsibility as he looked into the future and probable young family and Anne as a provider of all that was domestic. They would not partake in sex yet, not past a kiss on the cheek. Anne knew that she was not ready.

A tradition known as *shivaree* could not be ignored though, as it was expected. It was a given that wedding guests would return uninvited to the home of newlyweds, banging pots and pans into the wee hours of the morning. The practice often involved shooting guns and forcing entry into the matrimonial residence - anything to mischievously disrupt the presumed wedding night activities of a newly married couple. Anne and Jean were spared from this and they only had to put up with a little rattling of pots and pans outside their window.

They were happy to have missed out of the more embellished hazing to induct them into the community of other married couples. They merely curled up tightly, with knowing that the shared warmth of their bodies was an indication of what the future would hold.

Anne had planned their first large meal for over a year. Her mother had trained her well, she had scouted the neighbourhood for supplies and when the time came, she was ready to cook for Jean and his parents.

It was a success. Anne had practiced two recipes. One was a maple sugar pie, which was a custard-like dish of maple syrup thickened with cornstarch.

The second was her favourite. Anne felt confident that she could serve her husband well as was to be expected - with her maple syrup dumplings. Jean helped Anne in the kitchen often, a rare thing in a land where women were chattels.

They often picked wild strawberries and then put them on slabs of wood to set in the sun to dry. They later would eat them with maple sugar, in the winter, when fruit was not available.

William and Michèle gave them the space and time that they needed. Michèle was keen to teach any details about life that Anne may have missed, but they allowed the young couple to grow into their tasks and become self-assured, willing to toil and ready for any uncomfortable happening.

On Christmas after their first year their home was well stocked with both wild game and the food that their mixed farming had produced. Anne cooked a splendid meal of roast venison with boiled herbs. She followed it with a dessert of a pudding of corn flour, lightened with eggs, which was also sweetened with maple sugar.

Jean understood that Anne was still a girl in so many ways, the least of which was physical. The rules of consummating a marriage were lenient. It was not unusual to wait for sex until a more advanced maturity, even until four or five years after a wedding. As a male, in this century, he had no expectations from his young bride. Active sex could evolve slowly.

It did - and both Anne and Jean enjoyed a process that was outside the realm of casual dating. They became true friends and partners within their home life, which also included their work life. They were a married couple, but as if setting time aside for each other, in a dating or scheduled pattern. Finally after playing and bantering about, they finally consummated the marriage.

Anne served a venison course on many festive holidays, but on the third Christmas, this splendid meal was created by a very young girl – now a mother to be.

***

Anne enjoyed her housework duties and she was very aware that throughout her lifetime a never- ending schedule of labour was to be her life. However, she was of a new generation that had become aware of more worldly things. Some seemed incidental. Others were of a community changing. Knowing that Quebec City was being provided with cobblestone streets seemed a true awareness of the world. But, other things mattered more to a young girl's mind.

Through visiting with older girls at church and hearing rumours about the few elite women that would be seen only on occasion, she knew that it was true that the ornate dress of an aristocratic lady made any physical activity impossible. Life was meant to be that way.

In contrast, her country women's cap, thick dress and wooden clogs were designed to protect her from dirt and enable her to work simultaneously in rain, cold, mud and manure. She knew her lot and accepted it.

Women's clothing would not change and it still began with a chemise, a nightgown-like undergarment, usually of white linen. It would show slightly above the bodice or through the sleeves, but it is underclothing. She now wore it all in a manner that by Jean's perception was very appealing.

The next garment allowed was a kirtle, a one-piece sleeveless dress, and over this a gown or overdress with bodice attached to a skirt. The gown opened up the front and laced together. Sleeves could then be attached by pins. Even the poorest women would be expected to have a little *pin money* for those so-necessary pins to keep her clothes together.

Anne observed that even inside, she needed to wear her skirts above her ankles, often as high as mid-calf. She couldn't afford to be tripping on them around the hearth!

Noel Pelletier was the first Canadian born descendant of this Pelletier family from Tourouvre, France.

Anne was now 17 years old.

Anne's daughter born later would be named Anne.

MARRIAGE A LA GAUMINE

The scene is one of rural tranquillity in the New World, however, sometimes there is an excitement within the traditional Sunday Mass. Their church is small by any standards, but it suited the needs of their new found community. The date is August 19, 1650.

One member becomes bored with the Latin discourse of the Priest. He leaned over to speak to his peer, a man from up river: "Antoine has become an established habitant. Françoise Louise Morin, his long time sweetheart, has already moved in with him."

The second member smiles knowingly and shares information: "I heard that they are going to have their *marriage à la gaumine* today."

It was a good rumour. The first member was leading up to that possible fact: "They are close to the altar, up there - in the third from the front row. It's maybe today!"

A man in the row in front of them turns around to join in the conversation. He does so with an explanation: "It's a process based on strict interpretation of a Papal ruling. The marriage requires the church's blessing."

"Yes, I know," states the first member with excitement. "*Marriage à la gaumine* holds that people who wished to marry can attend a regular church service and announce at the end of it that they regard themselves as married."

His wife states: "They must stand up though. They must stand up in front of us, so we can recognize them as a new couple."

"Well I think they are going to do it!"

Another member in front of them whispers something inaudible. The priest turns and looks out on them and tilts his head as if questioning. He then raises his eyebrows. They stop talking. The church service always in Latin, carries on.

Antoine and Françoise begin to stand, however, they quickly sit down again when the priest turns to face his audience. The trick is to not get caught. The priest speaks briefly, then again turns his back to them. He again prays in the direction of the Altar.

Antoine and Françoise stand, and grasp each other's hand, then turn to the congregation. The couple are smiling with glee.

A number of the church members smile and make a point of nodding to them. The service carries on with the priest oblivious to any traditions.

Only minutes later, after the Mass has concluded, the members are gathered in the churchyard area. It is a beautiful summer day, with the sun also blessing the marriage.

The first congregation member walks quickly over to Antoine and his new bride: "Antoine and Françoise - congratulations!"

Antoine beams with pleasure: "We are husband and wife! Thank you."

The Second Member speaks to a small group on the edge of the clearing. "I saw them. They stood proudly and smiled and even waved at us as the priest attended to the mass with his back turned."

"All consider this the announcement of alliance," is a reply.

The man from the row in front of the two joins the group: "The priest expected to remind the newlyweds that their wedding bed would someday be their deathbed, from where souls will be taken to be sent before God's Tribunal. In relating to this, he would have declared that the bed is for children to be conceived and born and is not a place for pleasure."

His wife says: "So it's wonderful that they had a marriage à la gaumine instead. Today is perfect."

The second member only laughed: "We all like pleasure. It is good."

He then smiles with satisfaction: "Yes, of course. They will have a long and wonderful life." He pauses: "But it's unfortunate that for this very reason Antoine's marriage to Françoise Morin can't be considered legal by some. I personally agree with it though. The best to them!"

The discussion continues: "A more wonderful life you say. That is the reason for it as there is too much control! Even the pleasure of our beds may be a changed tradition here far from France."

Such are the conversations of the first few years in this the new land. It is with an optimism of what the *New World* may bring.

DRUNKEN CANOEING

Montmorency Falls, with two Pelletier farms above to the left.

Throughout history it was known that imbibing while traveling on the waterways, or even on the trails with mules and a wagon - was always dangerous. A tragedy was to be a part of the Pelletier family saga.

Michèle, William, Anne and Jean are standing on a beaten trial, in front of the farm owned by Antoine. They are with Antoine's wife, Françoise. There are many improvements including a small barn and fencing on her farm, but it is not a consolation on this day. It is October 2nd, less than two months following the informal wedding of Antoine and his bride.

Michèle is weeping while she spoke: "We all now know that Antoine has died as a wonderful man. He was drowned as his canoe overturned on the Montmorency Falls, but he would have wanted to be known to die that way. Not in his bed as a sick man."

She turns to Françoise: "Your farm is only a stone's throw from the upper head of the falls. It's dangerous at the best of times."

"He was returning home by canoe. He only had a few drinks. He always did that on Saturday night. He liked to get together with his friends," explained Françoise.

Michèle attempts to say the right thing: "He wasn't concentrating, that's all. He would have often used the river as transportation. He was used to it."

Jean is also attempting to say the right thing, but is able to say it exactly wrong: "Yeh, being drunk and visiting by canoe could easily have done it."

Anne seemed more caring. "We are so sorry about your great loss. He was a good and gracious man. The issue is not over-exuberance while imbibing and travelling. We all care deeply."

William needs to take charge. He speaks to Françoise, about the significance of being newly widowed: "As you didn't have a formal marriage contract, I now own one-half of Antoine's land. But please be sure that I'll now do the proper thing. I'll buy out your widow's half of the property as if you were married."

He paused, not wanting to hurry the conversation because of the circumstance. He looked around as is to observe the surrounding forest, just taking his time.

He added: "You were after all married *à la gaumine*. I accept that completely."

Françoise attempts a little smile: "I couldn't ask for more. I would have to pay the costs each year. I can't work the land by myself."

Michèle follows her husband's lead. As a wife she knows what would be important in the death of a husband: "Seigneurial fees are due once per year - on the day of the Planting of the Maypole. We will take care of it. You can relax without worry for awhile now."

"Yes. Life will go on," said Françoise. She accepts the reality of it all.

Michèle and Anne insist that she will come to dinner the following evening. Françoise agrees.

William now owned both his land and that of his late brother Antoine. He legalized this situation in June 1653 by requesting an act of concession form, from Seigneur Robert Giffard - which he received. The Seigneur in return was guaranteed production from Antoine's farm.

FAMILY

"Habitant Interior" by Horatio Walker

The celebrations of marriage, baptism and the grieving of death exists in harmony, all within the same building, that of the local church. It was a cold day In 1665 and the entire community is in attendance for the funeral of William (Guillaume) Pelletier.

The priest gives his perception of the life and all that might be important to the deceased: "In 1654, WIlliam sold his brother's former property giving a goodly portion to Françoise Morin. In this he was a gratuitous man."

"He had become a master carpenter and beam-maker. Having achieved success with this craft, William was instrumental in the construction of Chateau St-Louis, the governor's home in 1647 and of the parish church in 1648. The Ursuline Sisters in Quebec had made the detailed notation of this."

"At the age of fifty-nine, on Tuesday, November 27, 1657, William Pelletier died. He had spent 16 years in the colony."

The priest then gives a summary of the second part of William's life: "On August 9,1653, the population of the region of Beauport had shown their trust in William Pelletier by naming him vice-mayor, responsible for the economic interests of the inhabitants with the *Communaute des Habitants.*

William Pelletier will be buried tomorrow in the Côte de la Montagne cemetery at Quebec City."

* * *

The same church is revisited for a celebration of death eight years later, on a cold autumn day in 1665. It is the funeral of a very strong woman, that of Michèle Pelletier. Later the church family stands in the churchyard visiting and paying their respects to the surviving family, that of Anne, Jean and their children.

Jean speaks to his long time friend Paul: "It was wonderful that my mother, Michèle had stayed living with us at the Beauport farm. She was seventy-three when she died."

Paul says: "She lived a good life then. She toiled well and hard. Father Henri de Bernieres, curate of the cathedral of Quebec, presided at her funeral. That holds an importance to us all."

Jean wants to share his feelings: "For over five hundred years now, it has been a tradition that the wife of a craftsman, guild member or farmer, would work alongside her husband with equal purpose. My mother Michèle saw that as her sole purpose. She did it all. The last eight years or so without her husband were the hardest for her."

Paul is earnest: "She'll be happy with God."

Jean continues: "Throughout her lifetime she had a good never-ending schedule of labour. The work of ploughing was left to us but my mother helped gather the harvest - and she worked at other tasks to her last days."

Louis joins them. He had heard at least a part of Jean's comments and added: "Michèle Pelletier had looked after the family's animals - the hens, pigs and cattle. She shared her duties with Anne as her equal partner."

Paul asks: "Did she become a spinster? The spinning of thread was traditional for older women."

Jean bows his head in remorse. He had never wanted this type of conversation and wished it never happened. He repeats: "She did it all."

Louis asks: "Your mother-in-law, Françoise, Noel's wife, also died this year, as a result of an accident?"

Jean simply states: "Yeh." He pauses, looks down and walks away from his friends.

Paul turns to his friends: "William and Michèle Pelletier served New France without question of motivation, resources or usury. Life existed here in a changed form. To them it represented opportunity."

Louis adds: "But we are all cynical. Jean and many of us consider our future to be completely controlled by leaders living far from us - in France."

Paul continues: "Is it not apparent that everything political is decided by the toss of a coin, or by banter made over wine and feasts -- even with Champlain, remember?"

"True," states Louis. "Even important issues relative to Royal Ascent and government is by way of either rumour or misrepresentation of fact - at best second rate. We never know what's true."

Paul says: "With our attitudes about all of this, we all share not just a little in common with the personality and character of Jean's Uncle Antoine."

Louis summarized: "We are all alike here."

BLISS

"The Chores", by Cornelius Krieghoff

Jean and Anne are sitting in front of their rock fireplace. It has all of the ambiance that one can expect for a close couple - in any setting and in any period of history. They are content with what they have. Jean still remembers the land that he left so far away and the conditions that motivated the journey. He also is trying to reconcile his homesickness for the now distant land of France.

Jean says: "We can now rely on produce from our gardens of corn, a patch of barley and an acre of wheat. Life is good, is it not?"

Anne smiles and nods her head in agreement: "It is very good. My clothes are woven and dyed bright colours for dresses and scarves. They could never be bright before. Rushes are now used for mats and bags."

Jean adds: "My hunting suit is made of deerskin and it will last forever. I also learned an application from the Micmac Indians for using balsam gum for wounds, red ochre for insect bites and hemlock tea poultices for bruises and sprains."

"It is all that plus all that you learned since our marriage, Jean." She smiles.

Jean continues ignoring her too subtle reference: "You know, I had brought my ice skates. They were a sharp utility piece if we needed it. They could be re-moulded into knives or utensils. But, I kept them as skates."

"We need to use them more."

"You know, Anne, small frozen areas can still be cleared of snow just like below Montmorency Falls. I love the way you skate with your full skirt flaring into the wind. It's worth it to dress up for the occasion."

Anne is the one that kept them organized as a couple: "Jean, you were going to tell me about the new bonus payments."

Jean didn't mind her changing the subject as he had completely forgotten to share his new information. "If we produce a greater number of babies than had been expected before, there's a bonus paid. After ten children, three hundred livres is paid per year. With twelve, we're paid four hundred livres per year."

"Well Jean, you know I always loved my work of making children!"

"Anne, I love to make you work." He smiles. They are finally thinking alike.

* * *

They were enjoying the moment, however a decision to not pursue the three hundred livres was later specific. With nine children they would not have to be obedient to church and state, but sexuality remained important to them their whole life.

As they relaxed enjoying a pleasant evening, they discuss issues brought to their attention. Some of it was brought to them by the visiting priest and some was information shared by their few neighbors.

Anne said: "The European based population of New France is now twenty-five hundred."

"It's no wonder. Jean adds, "In France a peasant can't even look up from his work for the pleasure of acknowledging a neighbour walking across his field. Here they can stop work and visit."

Anne was reflective: " I know that this passing the time of day allows a break. The bones and muscles need that."

In their barn were two long-horned oxen. They usually stood passively in half-door stalls facing outward as if promising hard labour, or even just wanting attention. When passing, Anne often reached out and petted one of them between its horns.

At one stroke of petting a domestic cow would normally shake and toss its head away to prevent a further touch. But these oxen would put their head up toward her hand as if seeking more attention.

Dogs do that instinctively and sometimes, even cats do it. The two huge beasts with long horns munched away while her children also often petted them, crawled on them and rode them. Like most children Anne had ridden an oxen as a child, often petting it. They always became a favourite pet.

There was also the leisure of a summer's stroll. Anne and Jean's neighbour is two kilometres away and as habitants they are now easily capable of traversing that distance for short visits - strolling through a picturesque valley.

A different time of the year could also be enjoyable. Snow and ice is seasonal with winter travel being easy, but it required a lot of preparation. Dressing for the cold is a matter of survival - frozen bodies were too often found on the St. Lawrence river banks. In spite of this, they endured and found pleasure in winter pastimes.

LIFE

Daily life was not easy at the best of times, and it also had its extreme hardships and dangers.

Anne and Jean strolled through the fresh morning air. Seeing their neighbour working alone in the field, they joined him.

Relatively speaking, George is a new immigrant. Anne and Jean enjoy sharing experiences with both George and his wife. They smile, share thoughts about the weather, but as is often the case now, they begin more earnest discussions. George is aware of the Indian threats.

Anne has said her hello and she stands aside, intending to leave the men to speak, just enjoying the spring air.

The conversation turns more serious.

Jean states his newest observations: "The Iroquois are still a constant menace. With our homes separated, it's impossible to aid each other in times of attack. We used to live in close knit communities for a reason. Now we can be slaughtered before anyone can help ."

Anne offered from a few feet away: "Sometimes we even lived in forts."

George searches for solutions: "So, with all of the Iroquois assaults more fortified stockades have to be built where we could take refuge with livestock. No?"

Anne walked from a few feet away and joined in: "It's not just the livestock."

"So, when they attack it exposes the vacated fields - as we have to abandon our homes and fields to their wasteful destruction," said Jean.

George looks worried.

Jean shares more of his observations: "The few attempts to have everyone live with farms that radiated out like the spokes of a wheel out from a town, weren't successful."

With both knowledge and confidence Anne adds to the conversation: "That's an old European fashion. We prefer river frontage, living apart, being lords of our own small domains – but it's dangerous."

George says: "I always feel like they're hiding behind the logs and trees surveying habitant life. But only a few uprisings occur, so we can probably carry on life as usual."

Jean almost agrees: "Probably, but the warriors of the powerful *Five Nations* of Indians held a powwow at Lake St. Pierre, and declared war on us."

"But the Huron. They seem to be friends?" George asks.

Anne smiles with a more positive reaction: "We acquired the habit of smoking tobacco from them. I guess that's real friendship. They grew the crop along the St. Lawrence River and we've now begun to cultivate tobacco ourselves."

George looks about at the nature of his new farming area and relaxes a bit saying: "Maple trees are a source of sugar as each spring the sap runs freely. We learned that from the Huron."

Jean adds: "Yes, learned from the Huron. We learned how to tap by cutting a diagonal incision in the trunk. In the lower end of this incision, they always placed a concave piece of bark, which piped the sap into a hollowed log. We do that as if we always knew it, but we didn't."

Anne wanted to make sure George was aware of the process and says: "After the sap is gathered and boiled in a large kettle over an open fire, the maple sugar is then formed into cakes."

George laughs: "And you survived well!"

George pauses. Frowning now, he has more serious thoughts to share: "I'm told that several hundred Huron, as refugees from the Iroquois attacks, have settled on Île d'Orleans. They had been some thirty thousand people. Measles, smallpox, and slaughter by the Iroquois had brought them down to a small band there."

Jean states: "The Iroquois captured eight settlers at Beaupre only six miles from here. Seven more were taken from Île d'Orleans. They were all killed."

"Remember, I just came from France," says George. "There it's never good. It's another world there now. Louis XIV is king and the court of Versailles is his world. He has created Roman art and the ideal architectural forms of antiquity. No lifestyle could be further removed from the realities of life here in Canada. But even with all of that, he can also be ruthless."

Jean always searches for new information as his world is one of utter simplicity: "What else can you tell me? I can't understand it really."

George says: "It's not the king, but Cardinal Richelieu who understood French lands abroad. He seemed to be our friend and the recent news of his death should be mourned. His successors may have an attitude of complete indifference, which will be an even greater threat to us. We needed his leadership."

Anne smiles knowingly: "But we need to live our lives by our own control. Don't you think?"

There is no direct answer. They are happy to discuss their crops.

* * *

Anne and Jean enjoy the quiet times. They could sit by their fire with the children asleep or often they would busy themselves with sewing, the cleaning of utensils, or the cleaning of a musket. It is a time for good conversation..

Jean passes on the news of the community to Anne: "The Company of One Hundred Associates has been dissolved."

Anne asks: "Were they the ones you spoke of when we met?"

"Yes, they were the ones that sent us over here by boat. It was their money. We were their investment."

Anne is interested, much more than when she was younger: "Does that mean that no others will arrive the same way?"

Jean says: "Probably. They had just sent the first horses to Quebec City. There were twelve. That was very exciting, but it may have been more of an excuse for a boisterous party. We didn't receive one. Not a single horse here."

He laughs as if it were a joke. He hadn't ever expected to receive a windfall such as a horse.

Anne says: "What's changed? With the company, I mean."

"They've come to realize that it's all a losing proposition here for us. They've now provided a bishop, a governor, and an intendant anyway. But no more. The population is way less than they wanted."

1666 Spring

Having shot a charging bear, Jean would retain the fur. Anne and Jean knew that skinned bear skins were ideal for cold nights. Anne and Jean worked together to scrape the flesh from the hide using two sharp knives.

Anne immediately stated the positive: "It's not that gory to separate the meat from the skin. I thought that it would be worse."

Jean replied: "No, the meat rolls off in chunks. That helps."

He separated one huge piece of meat, rolling it to the side.

"It's not that much different than cleaning fish. Only larger."

"Much larger," added Anne.

Jean said: "You have to be careful not to puncture the skin as you remove the closest layer of flesh. The fur is thick, but the skin is thin."

They sharpen their knives many times and continue to work removing all of the flesh and tissue. This process took one full day of careful scraping.

Anne prepared a tub of water, putting it near the fireplace to heat. She was following Jean's directions.

"Anne, we'll now place the hide in the water. We'll take turns working the skin with a brush for one hour.

Anne said, "I know. That will remove the grease from the hide."

In repeating the washing process a couple of times they had finally removed all of the grease from the hide.

Jean had no choice but to shoot the bear, but he made a statement as if he had. "Spring bears usually have fuller pelts, but fall bears have a higher gloss."

Anne replied: I'm content with as full of a pelt possible and you had shot the bear in spring."

Jean said: "We have a beautiful bear skin rug."

***

When it is yet another day, another visit and time for another parting, Jean speaks to Paul, his close friend. They sit in Anne and Jean's cabin enjoying a pipe together.

Paul says: "I'm excited about hearing what you want to do with your property here, Jean."

Jean explains: "I'm leasing it out. As I've inherited my father's half of the homestead, I'm fortunate. My mother gave up her half also to me. But, our homesteads are interesting. We receive the right to farm; however, we gain the obligation to produce a minimum for our seigneur and church."

"You have two acres. In this day you need more than that in order to make a living," states Paul. He is now more accustomed to the land and the economics from it.

Jean says: "Farms are getting bigger now. It's the times. But, I'm actually going to rent this land to both Guillaume Lizot and Robert Gallien."

They speak about other issues, often referring to their livestock. It was an evening of enjoyable conversation, food and drink. Paul is asked to stay and he is soon asleep on the floor in their warm bear skin rug.

A few days pass, always with an overview of contentment for the entire family of Anne and Jean.

With a welcomed knock on the door, Jean quickly opens it and acknowledges his brother-in-law, Jean Langlois. He gives him a hug as does Anne and they laugh at nothing in particular. A chair is pulled out to be set in front of the fireplace hearth.

Jean smiles at his brother-in-law and gives him the new information of the day: "I just gave Anne a description of our new property on Île d'Orleans. Two years have passed since we were given title to the land. Now I'll finally move my family there."

Anne added: "It's very exciting – in the St. Pierre parish, on the northside."

Jean's explanation was not actually needed: "In respect for her, we waited until after my mother's death. She wanted to live her last years here. But now we'll rent out this property - above the great falls. We now move to an island!"

The brother-in-law is pleased with the couple's resilience: "To live and to die, is often tied together."

Jean says: "The two acre frontage on the St. Lawrence River extends back to the middle of the island. The slope of the terrain means that the north bank will remain in view. It's as if we never left this bank."

They light their pipes from the fireplace again as a shared pleasure.

Jean continues: "The river is iced over now for access, and we'll continue to cross by boat almost six months of the year. It seems to provide all our amenities."

The brother-in-law shows enthusiasm: "You're on land title as 'The Goblet Maker' (Le Gobloteux). It's a hallmark of a new civilization, that of respect for passions."

Anne exaggerates: "We'll stay there long-term. Well, who knows about opportunity, maybe at least two years?"

They laugh knowing that a short stay could actually happen.

1666 Autumn

The first official census provided interesting details. The former European population had now grown to 3,418 inhabitants, with about half living in the towns of Quebec, Trois Rivières and Montreal. The census showed Anne as 24. Both Anne and Jean's ages differ from their birth dates, but this was normal as no one really cared about anyone's exact age. The census was thought of as just a government sponsored game.

An ambitious military incursion was launched. Six hundred local militiamen plus a hundred Huron allies joined the French troops. Along with Jean, George and others, they set fire to five large Iroquois villages. With this first glimpse of a new and more powerful military strength, the chiefs of the Five Nations decided to begin the process of peace treaties.

Later in autumn, after the crops were harvested and the winter firewood was cut, the entire Pelletier family returned to Quebec City to help build a cargo vessel. In the spring of 1667 it was completed. The proposition had been successful and the ship sailed to the West Indies, laden with staves, planks, cod, salmon, and fish oil. With the return of the vessel laden with sugar for these farmers, New France had established itself as a trading region.

1667

Jean turned 35 years old on the Île d'Orléans. The 1667 census reports that Jean's property has five acres cleared and that the family has a hired hand living with them, seventeen year old Guillaume Lemieux.

Sailing back and forth to the island in the summer was a difficult task. Jean could use the oars on his boat with skill, but the sails were another matter. His shallop, an open almost flat bottomed sailboat, required two people in stormy winds. As Anne quickly discovered on her first crossing, they would often change direction with the whim of the wind.

It was gaff rigged and Jean usually used only a single sail. But no matter how he tried to master it, they always remained at the mercy of the elements, working with or against the river currents. It was as if nature would decide on the fate of their crossing - as Jean would hoist the sail Anne held tight to the rudder with a forced smile.

After the arduous task of attempting to tack back home, for the last twenty feet of their voyage, Jean would pretend to finally be in perfect control as he guided the shallop towards the landing.

Anne would never remind Jean that her father had been a helmsman with incredible knowledge of seamanship, Anne often says - right after she takes her first steps onto the safety of the shore: "We did well Jean. We're getting much better at it."

1668

Anne and Jean meet Anne's brother, Jean Langlois in the field on his farm on the Island of Orleans.(Île d'Orleans). As they stand on the land and talked, it is obvious that Jean simply wanted to move on. It is a brisk, but beautiful winter day and Jean Langlois was quite joyful.

"I'm your brother-in-law, Jean. I wouldn't take advantage of you. You now have five acres cleared, that's a lot," he laughs.

Anne adds with a smile: "I wouldn't let you."

Jean is quite happy: "Okay but your buckskin suit of clothes has to be thrown in."

"I've been your neighbour for two years, will you tell me what is so important about my best leather suit of clothes? What about the currency? You have cash."

Jean says: "Bartering for the suit, along with the seventy-five pounds, holds with it a consolation. The Seigneur can't lay claim to a fractional ownership of a suit. No tax!"

Jean Langlois asks for clarity: "So I will now hold your first property along with the two adjoining properties that you bought last year?"

Jean says: "And I leave this beautiful isolated island of yours."

"You'll be returning to the original homestead in the spring - after the winter's thaw? is that when you can move?"

"Yes," Jean says: "to the original homestead at Beauport. The leases with Lizotte and Gallien have expired.

Jean Langlois is specific: "You and Anne had nine children. Seven were born at Beauport: Noel, Anne, René, Antoine, Jean, Charles and Marie-Charlotte. Two children were born during your stay here on the island. They were Marie-Delphine, who died four weeks after her birth, and Marie. But sometimes it's best to move on."

Anne says: "We have a wonderful life - sometimes."

Jean laughs as if to make it a carefree sharing of times. It is a mannerism that often worked for him.

Jean Langlois also knows that with a life so filled with tragedy, it was better to focus on birth than on death – and do it all with laughter.

Jean continues in the upbeat conversation of a good transaction: "Your ideas of life - and your suit - makes our transaction worth while!"

They are in agreement.

1669

In the spring Anne, Jean and their family return to the original homestead at Beauport. It is during this period that Anne at the age of 33, received the sacrament of confirmation from the bishop at Québec City. Her valid independence from the church had finally withered. She did as she had promised herself at a very young age - waiting until a later age to commit.

In only a few years Jean would sell the homestead to Charles Cadieu- de-Courville finally divorcing his ties with *land above the great waterfall* and his first home in this rugged country.

For both Anne and Jean, an emotional bond was always a part of their ties to the land. Even with the many moves they would strongly relate to the security of a home and all that it meant.

1672

Anne and Jean and the five youngest children move to Île-aux-Grues. The setting of *yet a* second island seemed idyllic to them, some of the people were not. They had settled into a cabin left by a habitant who had chosen to venture to the far west to search for his ideal settlement.

Anne scrubbed their wood floor often. This was just another day of labour. As she looked up from her duty, he was standing to her side. Startled she stood up as she said a nervous: "Good day."

He had a lear about him. Anne wondered why she was thinking about her great-grandmother at a time like this. *"We women always had a place to hide. It was that, or being mounted by the lord of the manor."* She set the thought aside: *"Ridiculous"*.

Jean was in the field, the rest of her family were out doing their minor chores.

She had not overreacted with her emotion of fear, at least not in her thoughts and state of mind. He grabbed her in an attempt to kiss her. He really did think that she was her husband's chattel - to be enjoyed as if he was borrowing a farm implement.

The next thing that she could not have planned is that she broke free from his attempt to hold her fast. She bent down, picked up the bucket of dirty water and slammed it down over his head.

Like a dog having been doused with cold water, he fled from the cabin. She would never see him again.

Anne's decision was to not tell Jean immediately about the assault by the *seigneur at Île-aux-Grues*. She could insist that they move for many other minor reasons. Later she would give Jean a list.

Anne then stated: "The cabin is inferior and can't keep out the weather. The land is not capable of providing nourishment for our family. And the island is very small with no game for hunting."

Jean made a decision in agreement. Anne had never complained. If she was unhappy now he presumed her reasons were valid.

He was told about Anne's motivations, only after they moved. Due to a time period involved, he could think clearly. If he murdered the seigneur he would also die. The community would not have accepted his logic. If he let fate evolve then perhaps it would be as God intended.

The *seigneur at Île-aux-Grues* did die from natural causes within three years. Having heard about it, Jean and Anne both felt vindicated. The could go on with their lives as they had planned.

Anne had been 35 years old when the assault took place. She felt closer than ever to both her grandmother and great-grandmother.

After just two years, Jean gave his second island property to Guillaume Lemieux, the former hired hand at Île d'Orléans. Lemieux was now Jean's brother-in-law, having married Anne's younger sister, Elisabeth Langlois Cote, widow of Louis Cote. Guillaume had always worked for little money. A few times they would give Guillaume a chicken to sell, or perhaps a few carrots for barter. He was a *peasant* by French standards. Acquiring the right to farm raised him to the status of habitant. It changed his life.

Brick Outdoor Oven

"Making sugar" by Cornelius Krieghoff.

THE DREAM

In 1655, while still living at Beauport with his parents, Jean and his brother-in-law, René Chevalier, had purchased a small parcel of land along the St-Lawrence River just below the high cliffs of the upper city of Québec. The parcel measures only 30 feet by 30 feet and was never put to commercial use, contrary to Jean's dream of building a store and selling pottery in a commercial venture there. The small parcel is eventually sold over two decades later to Louis Levasseur-Lesperance. Jean had given up on his dream of selling his pottery full time in an area of town that could be successfully commercial.

Of all the sales to *rights of use*, this is the only *freehold title* parcel to be had in Jean's entire life. He had referred to it as *our property* when talking with Anne, a fact that was unique in the time of a wife being just another chattel.

Jean stood in front of the lot, in the commercial section of Quebec City. René Chevalier, a good friend, partner and brother-in-law to Jean, had met him there to discuss the sale of their land.

René says: "This is a day for our final decision. Buying this property was more fun than its demise."

Jean replies: "I hate to sell it. We purchased it with a specific intent."

"We both know that you should be a full time artist. Your pottery is unique to all of the New World," says René.

Jean speaks in a wistful manner: "This was to be our selling outlet - our store. We talked about it as if it was to be our presentation to the worlds both new and old. It was grandeur. Maybe it was *delusions of grandeur*?"

René says: "It was a long time ago - we chose here along the St. Lawrence River, at the foot of Cap-aux-Diamants, just below these magnificent cliffs. We chose to dream."

Jean rationalizes to a certain extent: "The upper city of Quebec may never expand and this property may stay the way it is. But, I really would have preferred to live in Quebec City, create ceramics, and market them from a home that was commercial. It would have been perfect."

"It was a fleeting dream. Remember, the parcel only measures thirty feet by thirty feet. The money that we get from Louis Levasseur is money our families need," adds René.

Jean says: "It's probably best that my dream of commercial artistry is now set aside completely. I need to provide for my family as best I can. That is reality."

* * *

Anne provided an alternative dream: "Jean it's one of compromise. We have wonderful children and a wonderful life."

Jean often had often stated the same thing, in various ways: "I know we're happy, but I just wanted to focus on marketing my pottery in Quebec City."

Anne would counter with: "You needn't set aside your artistic values. The goblets have sold and they're appreciated by many."

Other realities exist. His neighbor, George and Jean would often share a pipe and this evening of conversation was no exception. Jean had shared a pipe with George accompanied by Marie, his wife, as often as they had visited Anne and Jean.

Upon hearing of Jean's sale of property, George said: "Selling your Quebec property gives you some freedom from the constraints of the rural system. It's like those of our fold who left to live in the west. They wanted more freedom. You wanted money and it's a very different time now, no?"

Jean laughs and changes the subject: "It's a different time, yes. Like the King's Daughters and their husbands, those west of us now account for two-thirds of New France. They've become quite a group."

George counters, as he knew of Jean's beliefs as they would often speak about the uniqueness of the time in which they lived: "We are learning. All of the population is changing."

"The Metis also likely outnumber the New France Colony, they're just spread over a wider territory," Jean jokes.

Jean loved this bantering about politics as he knew it: "I've heard news from France." He was laughing as someone about to tell a joke."

Marie questions him: "What news?"

Jean responded: "The Jesuit Priests are accused of baptizing more beavers than Indians!"

"You're kidding?" George laughed.

Jean became serious just for the fun of it: "Yes, their cardinal was paraded in front of the King. The King demanded to know why the records showed that beaver baptism numbers were so great!"

Jean repeated: "They had to explain to the King, why they baptised more beavers than indian." Jean was enjoying this.

"They provide though," says Marie. "I'm not very pious, but a special mass was provided by them last month. It wasn't a Sunday or even a Saint's Day. From what they have said, I've concluded that God won't grant us any more favours, unless we show Him our gratitude for other blessings."

"A wise spiritual path," agrees Anne.

"We gathered and prayed for abundance, at more than one special mass," continues George proudly.

"We prayed hard that our gestures would not be in vain," Jean speaks and roars with his style of robust laughter.

"Yes, we did." George was not entirely comfortable with what he considered to be blasphemy against the church.

"And it is properly noted by our illustrious administrators that the horse population of New France has risen to one-hundred." Jean understood that church and state were one.

George stated as if it would be possible: We are not to be one of the horse owners?" He was being sarcastic and making a joke at the same time.

"Ours is the wonderful world of oxen - peaceful, responsive, kind and domestic animals."

"Yes," summarizes George, "They are superior to the inferior and *fragile horse*."

"Yes, far superior," was Jean's agreement.

Anne joined in looking up from her sewing: "I like the story about baptizing more beavers than Indians - best!"

Marie was in agreement: "It is very funny, even though it is true."

They laugh again.

Anne, Jean, George and Marie enjoy their worldliness. To judge civilization seems strangely humorous to them.

SOUTH BANK

Family by Cornelius Krieghoff

Jean had held an open mind in his attempt to settle his family in the new land. It became obvious to him that as a habitant, he had to make tough decisions. He couldn't just accept the land that he was asked to serve on without some kind of evaluation. The existing hierarchy was not on the lookout for opportunity for the settlers as their vested interests were elsewhere. Jean's father had held a different belief. William was someone who would never question those in control.

In 1674, Jean and Pierre Grosleau are invited by Nicolas Juchereau to go to Grande-Anse to evaluate the property of Juchereau's deceased son-in-law, François Pallet. The trip to the new area stirs in Jean the idea of moving again to the newer territory of the *South Bank*.

Jean had met with Nicolas Juchereau for only a few minutes on another occasion. Now, the entire south bank In the Grand-Anse area had been ceded to Nicolas as Seigneur.

Meeting Nicolas and beginning with a conversation of necessary small talk, Jean says: "Your son-in-law died four years ago when he had just started to clear this virgin forest. Farming here would have been his dream."

Nicolas agrees and explains: "Yes. I know that this was a long excursion for you to view it, but among other things while you're here, take a look at this soil. With a five-acre frontage on the river gently sloped, it can be accessed and used easily for farming. By all standards it is a large plot of land."

Jean picks up and holds the black loam in his hand and looks about. Down below, the river had eroded the boulders into large flat stepping stones. They were running from the farm into the flowing waters. He can see the north bank of the St. Lawrence River in the distance.

Jean says: "By boat it isn't far – on a good day," He smiles enjoying the fact that it is a beautiful day.

Jean adds: "It's easier farming. And it's quiet here - safe. I tried another parcel. Only two years ago I left Beauport to travel down river. It was my choice, but the rural system there wasn't a fair one. It was to do with the levies discussed with the Lord of the Manor."

Nicolas agrees: "We must believe in the course we take."

Jean continues his saga: "I then tried Île-aux-Grues for three years. I moved there with Anne and the five youngest children."

Nicolas is a bit puzzled and inquires: "It's unusual to move repeatedly?"

Jean explains: "We serve on rented property, but no one seems to grasp that. Farming can be a system of usury you know. Our two eldest children, Noel and Anne, are no longer living at home. Anne, our daughter, has been married since 1670 and Noel since 1673. Both are living with their spouses in the Grande-Anse area. They'll be raising their family not very far from here."

Nicolas is not about to disagree with Jean as he had an obligation to succeed and a farm to unload: "You have reasons, which are yours to keep, and God's to trust."

Jean feels like being himself this time. He won't promise to be married to the land, when he obviously isn't: "I seem to be a man of strong opinions about freedom, and I'm a man who creates. I have my pottery. In short I am an artist. I prefer to simply create beautiful goblets."

Nicolas smiles. He gives thought to the fact that it all seems to be coming together and that perhaps this is to be Jean's last home. He also knows of Jean's family of hard working offspring.

Jean asked: "You've told me that good clay is also nearby?"

"Yes, much of it." He laughed. Now he felt confident.

Jean is positive: "Good, it is. This area includes the villages of Rivière-Ouelle, Ste-Anne-de-la- Grande-Anse and St-Roch des Aulnaies. It's a large area."

"You just have to make your decisions."

"And I can sell our property at Île-aux-Grues to my brother-in-law. I'm reckoning the farm would be their perfect marriage present. It can be a sale of convenience to both or us."

"So you will move to a final farm?" asks Nicolas. "Your nine children with their many offspring can now live and thrive here on the south bank of the mighty St. Lawrence River?"

Jean says: "Yes, we will. The farm can be ours. And this territory has you Nicolas Juchereau as Seigneur. You seem like a very fair man. When we have a census, it will likely show that my five acres have been cleared. I will prosper by all standards."

Nicolas is relieved. He knows that finding the first two settlers would be the hardest. "I think that the area will remain as remote as pioneering along this vast river can allow. The Jean Pelletier and the Pierre St. Pierre families will be the only two families within many miles."

Jean summarizes: "After the chaos of political struggles on the north shore, this can be a quiet time of enjoying family."

Nicolas speaks as a friend. He isn't condescending as a man in his position would often be and Jean is aware of that fact. "I've heard about Lachine, along the shore of Lake St. Louis, very near your former home. The seventy-seven settlers and their families with their peaceful high-peaked houses; were also hard working. I heard that on the night of Augusts 4, fifteen hundred Iroquois warriors attacked the village?"

Jean says: "It was a massacre and a night of torture of the worst kind imaginable – the night of the *Iroquois Revenge*. That black cloud of fear that had always hung overhead is now shown to be true."

"The river isn't a complete barrier; but it increases the distance," says Nicolas.

Jean looks about his new surroundings: "We'll be able to focus on life in a more peaceful community. We can build a road from the farm to carry our produce by oxen and cart to your mill..." His voice trails off and he adds: "It'll be a good settlement."

In 1679, census was detailed: Jean Pelletier at Beaupre 56; Anne Langlois (*sa femme*) 44, enfants: Rene 25, Jean 18, Marie 15, Charles 10, Marie 7, 1 rifle (fusil); 9 horned animals (betes a cornes); and about 7.5 acres of land under cultivation.

After a whirlwind of moves over the two decades, Anne believed she was now home. She was correct.

Jean Pelletier and his wife Anne, along with their offspring, did become The *South Bank Pelletier Family*. In the first year Jean built a salting shed, as later was to be a common practice on the south bank. Domestic meat, hunted game and fish could be salted and kept through all of the seasons.

They become more attuned to the use of the river and its produce. Their home is built with stones and mortar. The stones were gathered in the nearby hills and were chipped until they were rectangles. They were set one on top of the other to interlock. Three small open windows provided light and two separate doors gave them access and comfort.

They can see the river from their home; however, the choice of location is as far inland as possible, away from the winds that blew off the St. Lawrence River. For this reason the windows were also facing away from the river. Years pass and Jean and Anne relax in front of their hearth, built for such winter nights.

Jean is being wistful: "We have a new and wonderful life here." "We have much progress to be thankful for," follows Anne. "Good food and drink - and we're safe here on the South Bank."

Anne carries the premise onward with a knowing smile: "This is thanks to you, Jean, for hard work and sacrifices."

Jean was proud of his accomplishments: "Bread is now baked in large outdoor ovens, le fours Turgeon, which are shared by our families. We bake beans and tourtières. Our individual wood-burning ovens are made of hard packed clay and stones. Wooden roofs over the ovens keep rain or snow at bay. Masonry root cellars, embedded in steep slopes, are used for winter storage of vegetables."

"We eat well."

Jean smiles as he enjoyed their times like this. It was a game that they both enjoyed, that of communication: "In late winter, we enjoy listening to the roving storytellers and we have been known to often join them in dancing and singing."

Anne speaks with her usual optimism: "These free young men are worldly, if not sophisticated - even though they are French and recent arrivals here."

Ann wanted to raise a point and this was an opportune time to do it: "I don't mind that the priest joins us often. He has the gossip of the colony."

Jean says: "I remember, you finally received the sacrament of confirmation to the church at the age of thirty-three."

Anne feels that she had not been a heathen and did not wish it to be said that way: "I had hesitated for specific reasons. The church could control us, but being controlled wasn't as much of an issue as knowing that control was based on intelligent decisions."

"We held common opinions in this questioning of the church's logical control. We still do. We're habitants, not scholars; however, we were always aware that something was wrong with the system," agrees Jean.

Anne reminds him: "We didn't have a solution and don't now."

Jean says: "Pioneering with freehold land titles isn't available and the church is not about to be separated from government. There's no solution but to enjoy life."

Her response is well thought out: "We enjoy each other, Jean. Our family was kept at a small nine children so that I could live long – to enjoy us."

Jean frowns: "Our priest wasn't happy. I think he knew. But we made the right decision. I like the way we enjoyed us."

Anne smiles coyly and undoes the top hook of her blouse: "Sometimes you go on too much, Jean."

Jean says: "There is a reform movement known as Jansenism. It also contradicts the demands of the Catholic faith for their ongoing hierarchy. I don't understand it, but I heard that Jansenism what is also called the Protestant Reformation. That's from our old country. It's now being abolished here by order of the King."

Anne undoes the next top two hooks of her blouse and snuggles up to her husband and smiles.

She simply repeats: "Sometimes you go on too much, Jean."

***

Anne was enthralled with Jean's kiln, in all three locations where he had built. It needed no complex system and being built on their farms, she marvelled at what it produced.

She had asked: "You've simply dug into the side of the hill?"

Jean explained: "It's to give insulation. The design provided room for the ash to fall clear for the air to pass under the burning fuel.

Anne understood the reason that red clay was needed. It was that which produced the colour. Jean had discovered that he had no need to travel far for his supply. Red clay was within two hours walk.

Jean had explained: "When clay is heated, steam is driven off, leaving the clay rigid. The mature clay particles melt into one another.

They also often discussed that grey clays were fired to a darker and creamier colour. He would sometimes use the grey for variety.

Anne had asked: "Do you ever want to use a potter's wheel?

Jean explained: "Only one method is that of throwing clay on a primitive wheel. Due to the size and shape of most cups or goblets, a wheel isn't necessary."

Anne was alway complementary; "I hope you continue to dig your own clay. It is wonderful that you are able to dry, condition and adjust it with the knack of breaking, twisting and kneading the blocks of clay. I love your work."

Jean accepted her complement. "I am an artist." He added for humour: "I am very humble though. They laughed. These were the best of times.

DEFENSIVE BATTLE - FOUR DAYS

DAY ONE

In hearing of Jean's intentions to fight off the British invading from the south, Anne was in agreement: "Jean I understand the need to defend us by way of war. Guns are needed."

Jean responded: "They want our river for access to the Great Lakes. They also want to control the land north of our Great Lakes."

She smiled casually: "I understand that you have these not so enjoyable duties. But they are duties," she repeated.

In fact, she wished she could disagree, but being negative would be useless and she wanted to be supportive of a decision already made.

Jean answered almost as a pledge: "With the loss of Port Royal in Acadia, Governor-General Louis de Buade de Frontenac has ordered a preparation for siege here upriver."

Anne was reflective: "It seems that it should be peaceful now. The days of battles should be over."

Jean explained what he had already stated: "When the New England envoys delivered the terms of surrender for us, our Governor- General declared that his only reply would be *"by the mouth of my cannons"*.

Anne asked a question that she already knew the answer to: "And that involves us - you?"

"I am a young man yet. I have no ailments and I am needed," Jean paused as he knew the gravity of the situation. He might not be coming back alive.

He continued: "At 62 years old, and as a family head I need to make myself available."

Anne confirmed his assertion: "I know that you still hold respect as a leader."

"Paul, Louis and Pierre will join me. Others will follow. I have confidence in my friends."

Anne seemed to know that Jean and the local civilian militia was about to play an important part. Early the next morning she said good-by bravely, but with more apprehension than any time prior. His overnight hunting trips were never like this.

DAY TWO

In 1690, General Phips had left Boston with his fleet to attack. As he sailed up the St-Lawrence River, he sent raiding parties ashore to terrorize French settlements along the lower coast.

It seemed to be an assumptive attitude of the group that put Jean in leadership. Also it was logical as he was one of the few organisers. The men knew they needed a hierarchy in battle. They also knew that the probabilities were that a final battle was later to be pursued at Jean's home, on the South Shore.

The invading army finally landed at Beauport, Quebec, Anne and Jean's former community. Both Paul and Louis lived nearby and they protected their rights, having joined immediately. The foreign militia on the shore were constantly harassed by Jean and the local militia. This was not a formal battle as was the norm, but a repetitious shooting into the mass of the invading arming. Jean and his group had learned this type of malice well from the era of the Iroquoi uprisings.

Aside from the local militia harassing them, the battle for Quebec City was a disaster for the invading army for a second reason. Thirty-two ships came to attack the Québec City area, but only 5 were actually warships. Most of the others were merchant or fishing vessels.

Anne did not know of the outcome. As she looked out at the great river in the still of the night, she could not envision Jean's success.

Jean would not return this day - he had more work to do in battle.

DAY THREE

Never had General Phips encountered a fortress as formidable as Quebec. He would persevere throughout the night but in the end, he only created a minor resistance. He was about to limp back to his home base in Boston, giving up on conquering the Quebec fortress - but he planned to at least win on the rural South Shore.

Forewarned by coastal patrols, the settlers at Grande-Anse, under the leadership of Jean, prepared their defense. Now having experienced fighting together under the walls of the great fortress, they were about to repulse Phip's raid, this time at Rivière-Ouelle.

It was a clear summer evening and a group of men are either standing or sitting while watching patiently towards the wide expanse of the river. They are farmers, but they are heavily armed with hunting rifles. The first to break the silence questions their leader, Jean. He had served them well as a leader prior, in the year's past and the days before. They were still confident.

This question was asked by Louis: "So Jean, you said that Phip's raiders didn't expect us to actually fight, because we're not military?"

Jean is sure of himself: "No, they already burned a few homes down river, but General Phips thinks that somehow he'll just keep sending raiding parties ashore to terrorize our French settlements. He uses the idea of surprise. None of the other communities knew they were coming."

Jean looks around to see if all are listening, loudly proclaiming: "WE DO"

Paul speaks loudly also: "I guess it's another repeat attack on the town of Quebec. That's what they really want. This is just the start of their plan."

Jean is tired. He had spent the entire day and one-half of this night getting the logistics organized: "Yeh, that's their strategy."

Louis asks: "You organized this Jean. What else is will happen?"

Jean had been busy: "We have two fire boats up river. When the Bostonians attack, we'll set our guns ablaze from here. That will be the signal for the fireboats to be loosened."

Again there is a question: "Those are the rafts with the straw on them. They'll set them on fire?"

"That's the plan."

Paul speaks: "Well, we've waited a few hours now. It's been dark awhile so…" His voice trails off.

Paul has stopped speaking to listen. They hear the paddling sounds of two or more boats, all from the now crippled four battleships. In the moonlight they can see that they are loaded with a number of men. They all go silent and wait for the men to drop anchor and proceed to shore. The intruders lower themselves from row boats and wade in cautiously to shallow water, rifles at the ready, but expecting no resistance.

Jean waits and then it's time for his order: "Shoot them where they stand!"

Many volleys of shots are seen and heard from both directions. The two fire rafts are instantly set ablaze up river. They flow with the current as was calculated and then they collide with two of the ships anchored in mid river. There is a great blaze and a series of small explosions from the powder kegs onboard. Then all goes silent, but just for an instant,

There are then screams of the men abandoning the two ships on fire. The men from New England scramble to board the rowboats and they chart their course instinctively. They are rowing to the closest boat available. Their dead have fallen into the great surging river.

DAY FOUR

The full fleet of the expedition's ships, commanded by Sir William Phips, are now nearly destroyed by the fire-boats. Prior, he had suffered from a combination of the militia below and cannon volleys from the top of the fortified city. He also has now lost three of his warships from the cannons of Quebec. His and only one other ship is sailable.

General Phips aborted his secondary attack on the South Shore. He has met a resistance that to him is not believable. He presumed he was attacking a rural community with no fire-power.

In the early morning light, Jean and his militia are able to view the chaotic scrambling of the entire fleet. Jean shouts in excitement: "We did what we needed to do guys!"

Others are overjoyed as the remaining soldiers had rowed feverishly out of range into the night and had scrambled aboard their one remaining ship. Two of the three ships near the militia are still sinking.

"I'm glad that it's over. At least I think it's over!"

"We only seem to have one wounded. It's a bad wound, but only in the shoulder. Are you okay Pierre?"

A few of the men aid their fellow citizen up the small embankment.

Pierre gives them assurance: "I'll heal by spring, I'll dress the wound with a mixture of egg yolk, oil of roses and sap from the pine trees. It'll get better." He smiled bravely as he asserted his new knowledge of medicine learned indirectly from the French in his homeland.

Louis yelled: "Look at that! There they go and they only have two war ships left to limp back with this morning!

Jean was dominant in asserting: "Surprise was everything. They'll never attack again, not in our time."

Phips orders a formal retreat - to the safety of the Atlantic. As the other vessels were merchant or fishing vessels, he is willing to let them find their own way back. Only a few of them would make it south into Boston Harbour.

Governor- General Louis de Buade de Frontenac had been correct in assessing their ability to fight off the American-British. Jean Pelletier would stay on record as one of the leaders of the brave defenders.

Anne was overjoyed with the arrival of Jean in the wee hours of the following morning. It had been a long few days of waiting for her.

She had confidence in his ability in war, but wondered at the same time if she was simply naive.

More importantly, she was aware that he would not be in battle again. She was sure that now he would let his sons *do it* if necessary. With contentment, she now had her family safely within a short distance surrounding her on the south-bank.

Anne understood that for Jean, being an artist, designing and creating was his passion. It was not pursuing leadership in battles, being an administrator for Monsieur Jean Talon, being involved with the Jesuits, nor even farming, would initiate happiness for Jean. She understood that he was a potter, a wonderful maker of goblets.

NEXT GENERATION

The peaceful years go by and discussions about death, along with life, become less necessary. Jean and his son Charles often sit at the eating table where they discuss their business of farming. This is one such occasion.

Charles makes the statement: "Favouritism is not an issue with my inheritance. When we discussed it, the entire family was in agreement. It was me who emulated your love of this farm and this place - this is our utopia. My brothers understand that."

Jean agreed: "Often our choice for marriage and community dictates a move for younger brothers. In your case, also for older brothers."

Charles promises: "I have stated to my brothers that I'll someday buy my mother's share of the property. They find that important."

Jean replies: "Our farm has been fertile enough to provide food and clothing for all of our family even when most of us were together. The family, in turn, has been large enough, and possessed enough skill to run this farm.'

Anne took a break from her work, sat down and joined in the conversation: "We kept it free of debt even while meeting our seigneurial obligations. As with most families our lives are centred on the relation of family to land. "

Charles agrees simply and adamantly: "Yes."

The two men light up a pipe.

Jean agrees with Anne's point of view: "If the family hadn't been large enough, or capable enough, the farm would have an accumulating debt to our seigneurial obligations.

Anne agreed as she was smiling at Jean: "But unlike some of our neighbours we don't have debt.

She turns to Charles: "The following generation after you will also again scatter. Your children will move far and wide."

Charles said: "My brothers and sisters are already scattered. Noel, Anne, Rene, Antoine, Jean, Marie-Delphine, Marie and Charlotte.

Anne is concurring: "They're all over the place, but in solidarity with indivisible ties, we think of them.

It is Charles that summarizes: "Father, you have had to choose to give this inheritance among your children. My non-inheriting brothers might feel the burden of renunciation and react with signs of resentment." He is unsure of himself.

Anne kept in the conversation: "But, in each Pelletier generation, time will be the healer of such things. Family ties will endure."

Jean says: "Charles, you now live up to the expectations of your time and place in history. If the husbandry of this time seems applicable to both man and animal, it is not coincidental. Charles, you are expected to be a stud, no less and no more than a good horse or horned cow.

Anne understood a broader significance: "The goal of the hierarchies of both France and the New World are specifically built into our traditional culture."

Charles promises: "I understand. I know that I'll produce effectively."

He stood up proudly as if about to live up to that promise.

* * *

It is January 7, 1698 and Charles marries Terèse Quellet at Rivière-Quelle. They immediately return to live in the home of Anne and Jean as they will someday soon be the sole habitants of this farm.

In Anne and Jean's life, exorcism is the practice of casting out demons. The parish priest is thought to have special powers using prayers and religious material, sacramentals and set formulas - invoking God, Jesus, Angels and Archangels to intervene.

Anne's belief was specific. This is why she hadn't joined the church earlier in her life. She felt the bed was hers - and Jean's. It was not God's and it especially was not ruled by the priest. But she knew better than to voice her views in public.

In being a part of the exorcism of Charles and Terèse, Anne was assured that she had made the correct decision - for the bed to be that of pure love and enjoyment.

* * *

The priest arrived shortly after their arrival from their wedding, says his greetings and motions them all to go into the bedroom. As was normal Jean and Anne were now told to stand nearby. They are told they are participants, only due to relationships within the family.

The Jesuit priest was wearing a black gown called a *cassock* (*casaque*) meaning a long coat as his outer garb. Jean had read that the garment was mentioned in a decree by the pontifical council in 1604 - having learned this from his involvement as a *donné* of the Jesuits. Even though the attire was illogical in this wilderness the priest was extremely proud of it.

The priest pointed out that the 33 hooks down the front were symbolic of the years of the life of Jesus. It was bound at the waist with a cincture knotted on the right side.

He seemed to use the preamble of the description of his attire to lead up to more serious matters. The ceremony of blessing the large quilted bed is to be for the sake of the newly wedded Charles and Terèse Pelletier.

The priest begins speaking directly to Charles and Terèse: "Within the marriage ceremony, I have left no doubt about your duty as a couple. As we gather around your marriage bed, I bless your bedding grounds so that you may procreate as God intended. I will also do an exorcism, to ward off the evil effects of an especially dangerous curse that some enemy of yours may have put on the marriage such that it might be barren. This curse is known as the *nouage de l'aiguillete*.

The couple is holding hands. They bow their heads, dropping their hands to their sides, now with embarrassment, Holding hands is obviously for pleasure, a contradicion at this time and place.

The priest continues: "Marriage is the law of nature. As a priest and ordained exorcist I will pray."

The priest sprinkles holy water onto the bed, then makes the sign of the cross. He establishes his own obedience and the nature of their beliefs: "Lord, have mercy on us. Christ, have mercy on us. Christ, hear us. Christ, graciously hear us. God, the Father of heaven, have mercy on us. God the Son, Redeemer of the world, God the Holy Ghost, Holy Trinity, one God, have mercy on us. Holy Mary, pray for us. Holy Mother of God, Holy Virgin of virgins, Saint Michael, Saint Gabriel, Saint Raphael, All ye holy angels and archangels, All ye holy orders of blessed spirits, Saint John the Baptist, Saint Joseph, All ye holy patriarchs and prophets, with whom Christianity was founded, pray for us."

He pauses for a breath.

"May this bed be only for birth, sleep and death. May all other use by honour and faith be taken away."

The priest again sprinkles holy water onto the bed, making the sign of the cross with it.

He continues: "With the authority to command the evil spirits to leave this bed, I command you the evil spirit to come out and away in the Name of Jesus."

The priest continues in Latin: "De Exorcismis. Sancte Míchael Archángele, defénde nos contra nequítiam et insídias diáboli esto práesídium. Imperet illi Deus, súpplices deprecámur : tuque, princeps milítáe cáeléstis, Sátanam aliósque spíritus malígnos, qui ad perditiónem animárum pervagántur in mundo, divína virtúte, In inférnum detrude. Amen."

As the priest again sprinkles holy water on the bed and as he makes the sign of the cross, he repeats his Latin in their common language, in French: "Of Exorcisms. Saint Michael the Archangel, defend us; be our defense against the wickedness and snares of the devil. May God rebuke him, we humbly pray. And do thou, O prince of the heavenly host, by the power of God thrust into hell Satan and all evil spirits who prowl about the world seeking the ruin of souls. Amen."

It is now the last sprinkling of the bed in the sign of the cross and it is the final pledge on behalf of this marriage.

The statement is loud, specific and meaningful:
"WE WILL FOREVER DEDICATE THIS BED TO BE HOLY. Amen".

The priest now looks specifically at Charles and Terèse. His look is very stern. Jean and Anne look on knowingly. They understand that the young couple is being threatened.

Holding up his hands in an offering to God, the priest continues: "May this couple be fruitful and multiply. May they always remember their duties to procreate and only to procreate in this bed."

Anne and Jean are politely standing as far back as they can, just being able to see into the room.

The priest finally turns to the young couple to speak to them as two individuals. He finalizes: "The church may dissolve a marriage that produces no children. That would be on the grounds that evil had in fact made it barren. If you have a small family, retribution of time must be devoted to helping neighbors, however, focus is to be on the procreation and upbringing of children. Amen."

Charles speaks first as was to be expected: "Amen."

Terèse looks up lovingly at Charles. To her, this is a time that is as tender as the wedding vows. She is obedient: "Amen."

Jean and Anne are relieved that it's over, possibly with a reflection of why others such as their brother, Antoine, had chosen other marriage possibilities.

As the priest left the bedroom, the couple offers him wine, some tourtières and suggests a visit.

"Thank you, no. As you can appreciate I am now quite tired from the wedding ceremony. It's been quite a long day."

This is a welcomed reply. As both the father of the groom and as a gracious host, Jean logically replies: "It has been a wonderful day. Thank you Father! We can see you tomorrow at the festivities."

The priest shakes hands, bids good-night and leaves the cabin.

The newlyweds look at each other as if they are going to be up to mischief. Each gives a slight laugh and they retire back to their bedroom.

Jean and Anne retire to their own bedroom. It has been a long day but the three day festivities have only begun.

Shivarees are standard as they are considered to be a fun way of harassing newly weds, keeping them up throughout the night. This could involve at least the banging of pots. This was even construed as becoming a part of a wedding party for all involved. But in Charles and Terèse's case there will be no shivaree as the population of the area does not warrant it. It could be said that the population does not yet allow it.

While the exorcism of the bed was a known part of Charles and his family's history, - the event seemed only vague to Anne and Jean. They set it aside like it was an historical event - a tradition that was initiated by law and not by logic.

As with all of their children's weddings Anne and Jean shared a love that felt closer with each ceremony.

Such was Charles' first marriage blessing. He married again when Terèse died - and had fourteen children in total. His second marriage was to Marie-Barbe St. Pierre on January 12, 1711 at Rivière- Quelle, Quebec. Only six years would elapse between births in the two families. Even with two marriages, Charles had been a single adult for less than five years. He would keep his promise to his parents and to his community to produce effectively.

During the lifetime of Charles, on the south bank, the average man was 21.7 years old, and the average woman was an adolescent of 16.8 years old. Over half the population still consisted of teenagers. The youthful profile of the New World had not changed much.

Population growth came from births alone, as there was now little immigration. Intendant Talon had presided over the only big wave of immigration in the colony's history.

A FUTURE

Anne and Jean's home on the South Bank.
The rock walls and massive fireplace are original.

It is a typical scene here on the South Bank. Three farmers have met in a field and they are visiting. There is a slight breeze and the summer sun is hot. Pierre leans on his axe, as the break for good conversation is a welcome change from his constant cutting down trees in clearing where a field would slowly unfold.

"Hospitality is the law of every hearth. That I believe. But lately when our priest visits, he focuses on preaching sermons about the evils of local dances and entertainment," says Jean.

Pierre rationalizes, thinking that it is too beautiful a day to be negative: "In general we know how to enjoy life. Anyway we don't worry excessively about the church controls."

Jean says: "It's a dual track in life - and in love. All of the formality and rigid rules of the church - and even of the military, it all affects normal life somehow."

Pierre said: "You know the south colonies in the Atlantic area are caught in continuous warfare between France and England. But the war seems to be about a corrupt privileged class controlling the economics of France. It's not about us."

George states adamantly: "We'd be best unhooking ourselves from it. A hard-working class of people in France support the ruling class. They call them the Third Estate. That ruling Second Estate class is dependent on a tax on the land of the other eighty-five percent of the people. Remember, I just left."

Jean says: "I heard that in France there are often numerous taxes, all paid to a tax farmer. He creates them as he sees fit. Here we may soon have a tithe, the part of our crops and cattle yield handed over to the so called First Estate, the church."

George reminds him: "But in France it will always be worse. They're not parish priests such as here. They're just the new elite nobility of the robe. That's why I'm here – well - among other reasons, like being able to eat."

Pierre is usually silent as this is too much about world affairs. He is a habitant and he prefers his own type of rural focus: "We have freedoms. Our young men travel a few miles from their homes, in exploring other villages.

Anne has seen them visiting and has put down her hoe in her garden. She walks over to join in. She hears an opening in the conversation: "They look, of course, for where the girls are - that may never change."

Jean adds: "It was that, which along with the impracticality of dividing inherited property, that has produced the movement of people from one community to another. The Pelletier young men are about to become very scattered, as are your own sons."

"Pierre replies: "But we have twenty-eight thousand people in New France now. I've read that it's from new births alone."

"But we now call ourselves Canadian. We are not like the Frenchmen," says Jean.

Anne laughs: "Especially not like the French soldiers of Quebec City.

"Pierre continues: "Being under the control of a seigneur isn't as much of a problem when you weigh it against dealing with greater inequities.

Jean agrees: "It's surely a time of contentment. But we must be a good and subservient citizen."

"Contrary to what may be your new personal belief, rival kings and quarrelling governors do not care nor would they actually do anything of value for us," said George.

Pierre added: "You'll owe your survival to the often primitive, yet self-sufficient simplicity in which we live. Around livestock, we still wear carved wooden shoes, which are traditional in France. Walking in the manure demands it."

"As the men often toiled in the fields, I imagined spinning flax for the loom, churning butter and making cheese," said Anne.

The men were listening intently as she was making an unusual statement: "But the idea of *Women's Work* has progressed. I share duties often with Jean."

The seasons imposed harsh demands for labour, for seeds to be sown, crops gathered, fish caught and wood cut, all entirely dependent upon weather conditions. Cabbage, turnips, peas, beans, onions and corn were the popular vegetables, as they were all hardy and easily stored.

FRIENDSHIP

For Anne and Jean long winter evenings allowed card playing, dancing, shared pipe smoking, storytelling and singalongs. The spring and summer months would see many more celebrations of weddings and many new births. It was all about a sense of community.

They had sent word to Louis, Paul and Pierre inviting them for a visit. They are the same age, being in their sixties. The presumption was that their spouses were not available to visit. Firstly they possibly had to be occupied with their children or grandchildren - and domestic toil. Secondly, the cold winds of autumn would not have made it a comfortable journey across the river to the South Bank.

The evening began with the men sitting down to Anne's servings. The meal included her maple syrup dumplings, very much appreciated. Venison was the main course. For a desert, Anne and Jean had picked wild strawberries.

Jean makes a toast with a glass of beer: "To my father William - and to my family. To my wife - and to our family's future. And to you my friends. What we will have is better than what we had!" He waves his glass in the air in the manner of a great formal gesture.

Jean had learned to toast from his father, by imitating the world of France which seemed so far away. The scenario is not far away in time - it had happened before. The men, sitting closely around the table, respond with a reply to the toast.

They are not without optimism. "To the future." Smiles are the main feature of the room.

Jean waves as a reference to the venison. "We are able to hunt freely!"

Louis said: "In old France we weren't able to hunt, even in the vast forests of the king. We all remember it."

After the meal the men move their chairs to a semicircle around the fire. It is a process that is normal and uncalculated. Over the sharing of their pipes the conversation turned to the one person of their youth, who was missing. Paul spoke on the subject first.

"I've heard that Joseph travelled further west. Onto the prairies and even into the mountains that we've now heard about.

Louis said: "Did he ever marry? Did he have a family? Or do you know."

Paul answered: "I talked to his cousin. He had nothing but good news about Joseph."

They weren't in any hurry in conversation. The group was content to let the evening unfold slowly.

Paul continued: "Joseph married a Cree lady, beautiful, statuesque and respectful of him in every way."

Anne looked up from her sewing and asked: "They are from two different cultures. How did that work out?"

Paul was defensive in his answer: "They probably learned from both of their cultures." He had coincidentally given the specific answer before.

Jean was in agreement: "With gaining a knowledge of each other's language they can always thrive as a couple."

Paul was happy to report: "By all accounts they are happy."

Anne stated, not wishing to be contrary: "I'm happy for Joseph. He is a wonderful man. He will enjoy his family in the west, I'm sure.

The men reminisced about battles together under great duress. They laughed about good times and bad. They were sharing their thoughts candidly.

Mostly they communicated their belief in having left France being a good thing. They were proud of their community in every way. The communities on the St. Lawrence river were extensions of families.

Pierre said: "I guess we know every person and child on both sides of the river."

Jean added: "It was because we no longer were in France. We have visited often, like this wonderful evening."

Louis replied: "As our communities grow, we may lose some of our kinship."

Jean said: "What I meant was that here, in this new land, we are allowed to visit, we always have time for our neighbours. It's not all work."

Anne looked up from her mending and added: "You are like close-knit brothers. Many people here are."

Their concentration on nothing but the fireplace, with the comfort of the cabin, left them with a memory. To be cherished far into the future.

EPILOGUE

Jean was born in 1627 and he died February 24, 1698 at Rivière Ouelle, Kamouraska, Quebec.

Anne was born in 1637, and she died March 16, 1704 at Anne-De–La-Pacatiere, Quebec.

They were buried together at Rivière-Quelle cemetery.

It is a warm spring day and much of the snows have melted. As such it is easy for the neighbors to gather in the cemetery and visit after the burial service. Anne's coffin has been lowered and the priest has completed his service.

Old friends have been reunited, having intermittently returned to their roots. All of their journeys through life and surviving physically had been difficult, but enjoyed as was their choice.

Paul speaks first: "She was a wonderful woman of her generation. She made it past sixty years. That's unusual for a woman who bears so many children. She lived a long life, as long as a man."

"She was living with her son over at Anne-De–La-Pacatiere. But, they were pioneers here - one of the two first families in this part of the South Bank," adds Pierre.

Louis reads off of the tombstone: "Jean Pelletier died February, 24, in 1698." He adds: "He made it to seventy."

Paul felt he should add detail as a friend. "I know that he died at his farm at St. Roch des Aulnaies, in the presence of Robert Levesque, Francois Pinel and the curate Jean-Bernard DeRoqueleyne - only a little over six years ago. It's ideal when Jean and Anne can be buried beside each other like this. They were a close couple."

Pierre says: "Jean was buried in March, when the weather finally cleared. It was after weeks of a bitter cold snap and a long blizzard. We waited out the winter in order to dig."

Paul nods.

"That's a way of life." "A way of life and of death. We always wait submissively," says Pierre.

Louis says: "They have twenty-six grandchildren and three great grandchildren already. Anne Langlois Pelletier surely had accepted her responsibility for creating a new population."

Paul speaks slowly. He is being reflective: "She did it with pleasure and pride. It can be compared with the dedication of men going forth in battle. Our women are like that."

Pierre replies: "We're not to question the loss of female lives that usually end before the age of forty-five years. If they have birthed over six children, we are to expect it. No one can question it."

He is repeating himself as if trying to make it right: "Jean Pelletier had accepted the challenge of the New World, but had problems with it to some degree."

"He was striving for new thought and a newer system of freedom," says Paul.

Louis states: "He didn't die well off. He didn't carry a devotion to the soil, but he cherished both nature and the arts, and in that there is honour."

Pierre turns to Paul: "Did they ever settle that court battle in Beauport - in 1670? Jean became involved in disputes over property boundaries on the land closest to Montmorency Falls and the surrounding cliffs – at the top of the falls?"

Paul answers: "No, it was about the new purchasers, the ones after Jean - that's what the problem was. Court decisions were then made, appealed, counter-appealed, and the bitterness dragged on for six years until 1676. Jean finally won and sold his father's original land to Charles Cadieu-de-Courville."

Pierre: "So the bureaucracy did not rule in the long term."

Paul attempts to say it all: "Both Anne and Jean had accepted many challenges here in the New World, but had battled the system to some degree, striving for, or at least wishing for - change. I'm sure that's why they moved often. Both Anne and Jean wanted more than what was just given or allowed."

POSTSCRIPT

JEAN AND ANNE PELLETIER HAVE OVER SEVEN HUNDRED THOUSAND DESCENDENTS

The majority of the Canadian Pelletier families claim Anne and Jean as a common ancestor. Generations to follow Anne and Jean did benefit, without the loss within the farming system that had been founded on usury. But the most positive of all arguments for that early feudal system – is that Canada may never have been settled without that relationship of habitant to seigneur.

Their descendants are now scattered over five continents.

***

1901

Now only a few minutes' drive from Quebec City, Parc de la Chute-Montmorency is a beautiful park, entirely removed from the hostile setting of the seventeenth century. The falls are 83 metres high, making them 30 metres higher than Niagara Falls. An elaborate hotel was built on the site in 1901 and the setting is one of summer theatre, terraced cafés and a geological interpretation centre.

The park's boundary overlaps the eastern perimeter of the farm owned by Antoine Pelletier. William's (Guillaume's) farm abutted Antoine's to the northwest.

1998

On October 28, 1998, the Association des Familles Pelletier, Inc, unveiled a Memorial Monument with a plaque in St-Roch-des-Aulnaies, Quebec. It was in honor of Anne and Jean Pelletier's settling in the Grande-Anse area, situated at the Seigneury Mill site and museum, only a few kilometres downriver from their farm.

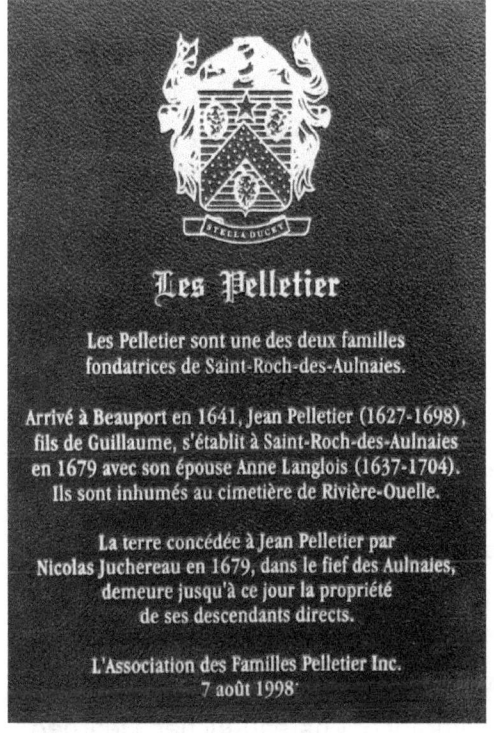

The plaque reads (English translation): *"The Pelletiers were one of two founding families of Saint-Roch-des-Aulnaies. Arriving in Beauport in 1641, Jean Pelletier (1627-1698), son of Guillaume, established himself at Saint-Roch-des-Aulnaies in 1679, with his wife Anne Langlois (1637-1704). They are buried in the cemetery in Rivière-Quelle."*

"The land ceded to Jean Pelletier by Nicolas Juchereau in 1679 (the seigneur), in the territory of the Aulnaies, remains to this day property of his direct descendants."

2003

My journey to France and the birthplace of Anne and Jean was not complete without a visit to the Louvre in Paris. Jean's goblets had become known as brandy-glasses, chalices, quaiches, rummers, tasses or wine glasses. I was able to visit the specific display of goblets from the 1600's attributed to the New World. In all of the original pieces, the potter's name was unknown.

I was able to easily imagine the unique probability of Jean Pelletier being the potter. I was elated at the idea of Jean's art work being remembered in one of the greatest museums in the world.

2016

In June I left Vancouver, BC, on a cross-country odyssey- a trip from the Pacific shores to the Atlantic's. I knew my route, but I arrived in the province of Quebec uncertain of the emotion I might feel. I was attempting to follow and if possible feel the warm emotions of my family roots. The site of the Pelletier family's first home at Beauport, was exactly 5,500 kilometres from the Pacific Ocean shore of my own home.

I began by visiting the archival library of Chateâu-Richer. I learned that in Quebec each village has a centre of genealogy that promotes ancestral pride along with restoring and preserving antique documents. The staff was helpful in letting me know what I could expect to find both here and on the Island of Orleans.

The William (Guillaume) Pelletier farm was not shown on the legal map of the area with his name; as the two existing maps only showed the original habitations. The Pelletiers' occupancy and registration was over two years after the original ceded *rights to farm*. William had purchased transfer of those rights. It was in that location that I had planned to stand and marvel at the first farm of the Pelletier family.

As hundreds of the Pelletier families have done before and possibly since, I slowly walked the farm area. My intention was to remain philosophical; as this was the first site on which my ancestors had also trod. However, as the diesel buses roared by, it was difficult to be overly nostalgic. *I could have gotten run over*. As a residential area it is now busy and is an intersection with winding feeder roads used by busy drivers. Their last thoughts would be to envision slowly plowing a single furlow through with an oxen.

I now felt compelled to follow the tourist *route de la Nouvelle-France* in these suburbs. My next visit was to *La Petite Ferme* and *Le Moulin du Petit Pré*. Champlain initially established *La Petite Ferme* in 1626; *La Grande Ferme* was created later in 1640 under Laval. As I traipsed through the area, I mused that this was where William (Guillaume) and Jean Pelletier most likely would have toiled for the Seigneur Giffard. They were hired as woodworkers here.

I now again paused and stood quietly observing the hills and trees. The buildings had been restored to the point of near-newness. It was terrain that my ancestors would have known and we could share this viewpoint of nature as an observation.

The next logical step was to drive the rest of this route and enjoy the architecture that is so specifically of Quebec and another place in time. It would be my observation that the same architecture exists in France, in the area of Jean's birth. That was a logical sequence as the architects of the time were the same individuals.

In 1663, Jean Pelletier took over an existing farm on Îsle D'Orléans from Jean and Nicolas Juchereau, Due to its size, and the hardship of island life, it is understandable that Jean would sell this farm on the island and move back to the mainland.

Jean, nicknamed *Le Gobloteux* was shown on the Îsle D'Orléans land use title when I searched for it. He loved to make ceramic goblets. Possibly none have survived, but this passion tells us that his thinking included a world outside of farming. Artistic flair was valued in the New World at that time.

It was a beautiful summer day and I enjoyed the moment. While taking a few photographs, I walked out on the properties and again contemplated the horizon. The view of the St. Lawrence River below and the surrounding agricultural land could not have changed much in several hundred years. Just as Anne, Jean and their family had done over three hundred years earlier – I finally left Îsle D'Orléans for the south bank. Unlike my ancestors, I used a modern bridge and a six-lane highway for that part of the journey.

Their next ownership as habitants was on the south bank at St. Roch des Aulnaies. Arriving, I was mentally prepared to begin a difficult search for the locations of four generations of my family. What actually happened took less than a couple of hours.

I wanted to look for the farm. In Eastern Canada, when a street is named after a family, there is a high probability that the name is of the original pioneering family farm. In such a small town it was easy to find *rue Pelletier*. Part of Anne and Jean's original farm was now a municipal park, so it was also easy to relax on a park bench and contemplate this third family location. Jean Pelletier had chosen a beautiful site and the farm ran gently into the St. Lawrence river.

Charles and Marie-Barbe's son Pierre Pelletier was born here in 1731 and he then lived here until 1757. His family also then *scattered*. After a time though there was nothing else left but for me to continue on in a similar manner.

I had no particular plan in mind as I was headed toward the next Pelletier farm along the southern bank. I stopped at La Seigneurie des Aulnaies. A museum of former life in Saint-Roch-des-Aulnaies, the visit seemed to fit perfectly with the day. I had been told about a Pelletier family monument but I hadn't yet determined where it was.

As I pulled into the parking lot, I immediately viewed two monuments, both just off to the side and both with a picturesque backdrop of flowers and shrubberies. One was emblazoned with the Pelletier family shield and crest with *Les Pelletier*. It had the logo of *Stella Ducet* inscribed beneath it.

Stella Ducet has various definitions from its Latin roots such as *Let the stars guide you* or *Be led by the stars*. It could not be more relevant in the seventeenth century. It was certainly a time of navigation by the stars.

The monument with the crest is an indication of a reward from the King of France given to Barthelemy le Pelletier, from seven hundred years ago, a time of more spiritual meanings. Important to the culture of France, it was indicative of bravery in the battle of Thouars, as he led a triumphant battle over the notorious English Black Prince and his marauders.

This memorial confirmed that I had visited the correct site at the municipal park a few kilometres back. Other information was available as I inquired further. The unique stone used to support the commemorative plaque comes from the farm "Beau-Prés" of Saint-Roch-des-Aunais, which belongs to Real and Placid Pelletier. They are ancestors of Anne and Jean.

The *Seigneurie des Aulnaies* was stated to be the only interpretation site that fully explains the French Seigneurial regime in North America. Unfortunately, the antique museum and building was built after Anne and Jean had lived in this area. They lived on their farm over one hundred years prior to its local references.

As I continued east, the next small town was Rivière-Quelle where my journey through the cemetery was similar to other discoveries. As usual, I did not experience much of an investigative search. The tombstone honouring Jean and Anne Pelletier was just a few feet to the side of the main gate. The rock tomb was large and the writing and family crest was clear with Stella Ducet emblazoned below.

Anne and Jean's lives were exciting, challenging, worthwhile, and creative.

They will always be a part of my life, my memories and my emotion.

APPENDIX

THE AUTHOR'S LIST OF SITES VISITED PERTINENT TO THE STORY

Chartres, Eure-et-Loire, France.

La Christerie. Home in Bresolettes, Orne, France.

Bresolettes Church, Bresolettes, Orne, France.

St. Aubin church, Tourouvre, Orne, France.

Montmorency Falls Park, Beauport, Québec, adjacent to the first Pelletier farm of 1644.

Jean's farm of 1663 at 693-697 chemin Royal, Ile D'Orleans, Québec, Canada.

The tombstone of Jean and Anne Pelletier, at Riviere Quelle, Québec, Canada, just off Hwy 132.

The Pelletier farm of 1679 to 1757, at Pelletier Street, St. Roch des Aulnaies, Québec.

The monument to the Jean Pelletier families at La Seigneurie des Aulnaies, Québec.

ACKNOWLEDGEMENTS:

During the research period, I was honoured to become a member and an accredited researcher at the "National Archives of France", a member of the association of *La Bibliotheque Généalogique* and had member access to the *Centre de Recherches et d'Histoire Sociale de Française*, in Paris, France.

Through this process I had access to the *Textes Sur Le Canada* and *Inventaire Analytique Colonies*, from which much related data was obtained. These were the original documents of communication both to and from the King of France. I am also thankful for access to the *Institute National de France* and the *Bibliotheca A Foundatore Mazarinea,* the oldest public library in France.

A few of the references in the story line are from the *Société généalogique Canadienne-française* in Lorraine, Québec.

Mr. George Pelletier, retired surgeon and a dedicated former family genealogist, verified my specific lineage information that had been handed down to me from near relatives, prior to publication of both *Pelletier Chronicles - 500 Years* and *Goblet Maker's WIfe*.

No other bibliography is appended as the historical data used outside of family information has become a matter of clichés. All learned facts over many years are found under titles too numerous to list. Detailed information related to family history may be found in *Pelletier Chronicles - 500 Years,* available in both eBook and paperback formats.

www.ingramcontent.com/pod-product-compliance
Lightning Source LLC
Chambersburg PA
CBHW061637040426
42446CB00010B/1455